GREAT WAR BRITAIN
LANCASTER
Remembering 1914–18

GREAT WAR BRITAIN

LANCASTER

Remembering 1914–18

IAN GREGORY, CORINNA PENISTON-BIRD,
PETER DONNELLY & MICHAEL HUGHES

The
History
Press

This book is dedicated to the late Brigadier James (Jim) Dennis. His committed work researching the war memorials of Lancaster, Morecambe, Carnforth and the surrounding villages, and the people behind the names on those memorials, did much to inspire the book and inform its content. His work was motivated by the desire to record as much detail as possible about the 2,700 people named on local war memorials 'so that their lives can be remembered in a fuller and more significant way for all time'. We hope that this book on Lancaster's experience of the First World War contributes to his aim.

First published 2017

The History Press
The Mill, Brimscombe Port
Stroud, Gloucestershire, GL5 2QG
www.thehistorypress.co.uk

British Library Cataloguing in Publication Data.
A catalogue record for this book is available from the British Library.

ISBN 978 0 7509 6825 6

Typesetting and origination by The History Press
Printed in Malta by Melita Press

CONTENTS

TIMELINE

1914

4 August

Britain declares war on Germany

14 August

5th Battalion KORL departs* *Lancaster Castle station for Didcot*

22 August

1st Battalion KORL crosses the English Channel on the SS Saturnia

24 August

First internees arrive at the Wagon Works, Caton Road, Lancaster

26 August

Battle of Le Cateau: first Lancastrians killed in action

19 October

First Battle of Ypres

1915

15 February

1st/5th Battalion KORL arrives in France

25 April

Allied landing at Gallipoli

7 May

Germans torpedo and sink the Lusitania

8 May

Nineteen Lancastrians killed, mainly at Frezenburg, Second Battle of Ypres

31 May

First German Zeppelin raid on London

25 September

Nineteen Lancastrians killed, mainly at the Battle of Loos

20 December

Allies finish their evacuation of and withdrawal from Gallipoli

*KORL: King's Own Royal Lancaster regiment

1916

24 January

The British Government introduces conscription

21 February

Battle of Verdun commences

31 May

Battle of Jutland

1 July

First Day of the Battle of the Somme: Ten Lancastrians die; 57,000 British casualties

July

National Filling Factory opens on White Lund

15 August

Twelve Lancastrians die on the city's worst day of the Somme campaign

27 August

Italy declares war on Germany

November

National Projectile Factory opens on Caton Road

18 December

Battle of Verdun ends

1917

6 April

The United States declares war on Germany

9 April

Battle of Arras

31 July

Third Battle of Ypres (Passchendaele)

20 August

Third Battle of Verdun

1 October

White Lund explosion and subsequent fires kills ten Lancastrians

30 November

Fourteen Lancastrians killed, the majority at the Battle of Cambrai

7 December

USA declares war on Austria-Hungary

1918

21 March
Second Battle of the Somme

15 July
Second Battle of the Marne

8 August
Battle of Amiens, first stage of the Hundred Days Offensive

22 September
The Great Allied Balkan victory

8 November
Armistice negotiations commence

9 November
Kaiser Wilhelm II abdicates, Germany is declared a republic

11 November
Armistice Day, cessation of hostilities on the Western Front

1921

18 August
Alfred Tyldesley dies of wounds, the last Lancastrian recorded as dying in the war

1924

27 November
Westfield War Memorial Village opened in Lancaster by Field Marshal Earl Douglas Haig

3 December
Lancaster War Memorial unveiled

ACKNOWLEDGEMENTS

We would like to thank the following: Lancaster Military Heritage Group (LMHG) for making the *Reveille* material available to us, and the King's Own Royal Regiment Museum, Lancaster for providing the record cards on Lancaster's war memorial to that project. The Documenting Dissent Project, run by Global Link (www.globallink.org.uk), with particular thanks to Caroline Morrison, Janet Nelson and Alison Lloyd Williams. Janet Nelson was also very generous in sharing further research, as was Pauline Churchill of the Lancaster & District Family History Group. Heather Dowler at Lancaster City Museum for her kind assistance with photographs. Mandy Stretch and Martin Purdy for their expertise on Westfield War Memorial Village. James Hayes for permission to draw upon his Lancaster University dissertation *The Enemy Within: Picturing, Confronting and Confining the 'Alien' in Lancaster and Morecambe during the First World War.* Bowerham Primary and Nursery School, Ripley St Thomas Church of England Academy, Lancaster Royal Grammar School and Lancaster Girls' Grammar School for access to school archives and memorials.

Ian Gregory acknowledges funding from the European Research Council (ERC) under the European Union's Seventh Framework Programme (FP7/2007-2013) / ERC grant "Spatial Humanities: texts, GIS, places" (agreement number 283850).

Ian Gregory and Corinna Peniston-Bird acknowledge funding from the Heritage Lottery Fund (HLF) for the LMHG's project

'Streets of Mourning and Community Memory in Lancaster' (FW-14-03372), that fostered our interest in the impact of the war on the communities of Lancaster.

Unless otherwise stated, all images are courtesy of Lancaster City Museum (LCM) or the King's Own Royal Regiment Museum (KOM).

Other image credits are to: Ian Gregory (ING), Michael Hughes (MJH), Corinna Peniston-Bird (CPB) and Lancaster Girls' Grammar School (LGGS).

INTRODUCTION

When census enumerators went round the town on 2 April 1911, they recorded that Lancaster Municipal Borough had a population of 41,410 people. In some ways the town and people they surveyed were typical of industrial Lancashire when the county, and indeed the country, was at the peak of its industrial might. The town's employment was strongly concentrated in manufacturing, particularly the production of oilcloth and linoleum. This industry was dominated by two family firms: James Williamson and Son (James Williamson II became Lord Ashton in 1895), and Storey Brothers. Waring and Gillow, furniture makers, were based on St Leonard's Gate and provided another source of manufacturing employment. Not everything was well with the town's industry, however. The Lancaster Carriage and Wagon Works on Caton Road had been the second largest employer in town after Williamson's until it closed in 1908 with a major loss of jobs.

Lancaster was not an entirely typical northern industrial town. As the county town it had a judicial role with the court and the prison, and it had well-established mental health facilities at the Moor Hospital off Quernmore Road and the Royal Albert for children with learning disabilities on Ashton Road. Significantly for what was to follow, Lancaster was also a garrison town: Bowerham Barracks (now the University of Cumbria campus) was the headquarters for the King's Own Royal Lancaster Regiment whose 5th Battalion, a Territorial Force unit (similar to the modern Territorial Army), was headquartered on Phoenix Street. A Royal Field Artillery battery was also based on Dallas Road.

Little could the people answering the enumerators' questions have known about what was to follow. From 1914 many of the younger men would be recruited, usually into the army, many into the King's Own. As many as 20 per cent of men in some age groups would be killed, many more would be injured or mentally scarred by what they experienced. For much of the rest of the population, life would carry on but would be far from normal. The town's industry and society were transformed as firms were moved to war production and women moved into jobs previously occupied by men. As you walk or drive around the town today, you pass many buildings that were part of this story: Bowerham Barracks and the other military sites were obviously centres of military activity; the Wagon Works was used as a prisoner of war camp; many of the mills and factories, now council offices, student accommodation, or disappearing under new housing, were used for the production of munitions or other products required for the war effort; many men enlisted at the Old Town Hall; and, along the streets of terraced housing and in the courts of the city centre, many houses lost men whose widows, parents, siblings and children had to carry on with their lives.

This book tells the story of Lancaster in the First World War. In doing so we draw together the military side, particularly the experience of the King's Own, and the civilian side with the impact of mass casualties, the town's civilian war effort, and attitudes to the war being key themes. In writing the book we are lucky to draw on two rich sources: the first is the records of the King's Own Royal Regiment Museum, and the second is *Reveille*, created by Lancaster Military Heritage Group and informed by the collections held by the King's Own, which provides a record of each Lancastrian killed in the war. The intention is to use these and other sources such as the local press to give the reader, a century later, an impression of how the global conflict affected the town and the people who lived and worked on the streets and buildings that modern inhabitants walk past every day.

1

Outbreak of War: The King's Own Mobilises

After years of escalating tensions, the immediate crisis that led to the First World War was triggered by the assassination of Archduke Franz Ferdinand in Sarajevo on 28 June 1914. Throughout July, tensions between Austria-Hungary, Russia, Germany, France and Britain rose and the complex system of alliances, combined with inflexible military planning, meant that the Austro-Hungarian declaration of war on Serbia pulled all of Europe's major powers, and many of its smaller ones, into war. On 4 August, Britain declared war on Germany in support of France and Russia, and in defence of Belgian neutrality.

The most immediate effect of this period on Lancaster was on its army units, particularly those in the King's Own Royal Lancaster Regiment which had been headquartered in the purpose-built barracks in Bowerham since 1880. Regiments consisted of a number of battalions which would typically comprise around 1,000 men and would operate independently of each other. At the outbreak of the war, the King's Own consisted of two regular battalions, two Territorial Force battalions and a Special Reserve battalion. The two regular battalions, the 1st and 2nd were based in Dover and India respectively. The Territorial Force battalions were the 4th and 5th Battalions. The 5th was based on Phoenix Street, Lancaster and recruited heavily from the local area, while the 4th was based in Ulverston. The Special Reserve 3rd Battalion also consisted of reservists and was based in Bowerham Barracks.

Colour Sergeant George Henry Brazier

Not everyone at Bowerham Barracks was suited for war service, either at home or abroad. The tragic tale of Colour Sergeant George Henry Brazier was no doubt not uncommon across the army in the First World War. Brazier had completed twenty-one years' service with the regiment, much of which was overseas in India, China and Burma. He left with a pension in 1911, but rejoined in September 1914, aged 42, to assist in training the men of the new battalions. He had been employed at White Cross Mill, and had also been at Bay Horse as a coal agent's manager: he was thus quite well known. With a strapped wrist following an accident to his right arm some years previously, unable to march, and with a possible drinking problem, Brazier was informed in December that he would be discharged as no longer fit for military service. On Tuesday 15 December his room mates at the barracks were awakened by hearing him yell, and they found that he had cut his own throat with a penknife which fell into the blood pool on the floor. He was admitted to the infirmary having demanded 'Why didn't you let me cut my head off?' and died shortly afterwards. The coroner found insufficient evidence to prove the man was of unsound mind, and suggested a verdict of 'Killed himself by cutting his throat', which was agreed. Brazier was buried in Lancaster Cemetery.

Group of reservists of the King's Own at Bowerham Barracks, 8 August 1914, about to head off for training near Plymouth. (KOM)

The records of the King's Own allow us a unique insight into the escalation of the opening days, weeks and months of the war. The weekend of 1 and 2 August was supposed to be the start of the annual West Lancashire Division Territorial Force camp which was to be held at Kirkby Lonsdale. In the lead up to the weekend it became increasingly uncertain whether the camp would go ahead as war loomed. The uncertainty increased when all oil sheets, which the men depended upon to protect themselves from damp when sleeping, and all blankets above war scale had to be returned on the Friday in preparation for the mobilisation of the Regular Army. In the event, the 4th and 5th battalions did travel from their bases on Sunday 2 August and arrived by train in Kirkby Lonsdale in heavy rain. At two o'clock on Monday morning, the news arrived that the camp had been cancelled and most men rapidly returned home. As a consequence, on the day before war was declared, a bank holiday, the streets of Lancaster were already full of men in uniform.

Ceremony and tragedy

The visible presence of the military in the centre of the town continued in the pending days. A battalion's Colours, or flags, are emblazoned with its Battle Honours and must always be handled with due respect and reverence. Colours had not been carried on Active Service since 1881 and it had become the tradition that Colours would be safely deposited in a public building for the duration of the hostilities. In the case of the 5th Battalion this was done with a very public parade through Lancaster, with the Colours being laid up in the Regimental Chapel at Lancaster's Priory Church on 5 August 1914. This was in preparation for the battalion being deployed, not to France, but to Barrow-in-Furness to protect the port.

The Colours of the 3rd (Special Reserve) Battalion of the King's Own were laid up in the Town Hall. The brief ceremony saw the Colours, carried by Lieutenants Watkins and Jameson, received by the Mayor, Councillor William Briggs. After receiving the

5ᵀʰ K.O. COLOURS TAKEN TO PARISH CHURCH AUG 5ᵗʰ 1914

Colours, the Mayor spoke to the officers and men of the 3ʳᵈ Battalion:

> In accepting the custody of your colours, I do so with the fullest sense of importance of the occasion, and all that it means. But I should like you to know that Lancaster is proud of its regiment, and wishes it every success, knowing that it will do its duty wherever it may be called to serve and do its best to live up to its great traditions with which its name is associated. My sincere wishes are that God may be with you all, and that you may safely return to receive your Colours back again.

The Colours of the 5ᵗʰ Battalion, King's Own, are 'laid up' in the Regimental Chapel for the duration of the war on 5 August 1914. (KOM)

The emphasis on men doing their 'duty' was reiterated in a more tragic context. One of the 5ᵗʰ Battalion's members who received notification of the plans for mobilisation was Private James Hall, aged 19, of Pilling. At around 10 a.m. on 6 August, his father, Richard, was working on his farm while his son cleaned his rifle. Richard heard a single shot and found his son lying over a cow trough, dead, with the stock of his rifle under his

Little is recorded of the 5ᵗʰ Battalion's time in Barrow, however, a foolscap piece of paper survives with instructions on how to deal with captured spies and how to search them for secret intelligence.

right elbow. As James was a 'keen religionist', it was surmised that he feared the possibility of having to kill his fellow men. Lancaster's coroner, Neville Holden, held the official inquest in Simpson's Tea Rooms the next day and told the jury that it was a serious case. A soldier's duty was to serve his King and country and it was an act of cowardice to take his own life. The jury was instructed to record a verdict of suicide. James Hall may thus have been the first British casualty of the war.

Whilst most of the men of the 5th Battalion were based in Lancaster, Morecambe, Carnforth and as far south as Garstang and Fleetwood, the men who were being mobilised at Bowerham Barracks were travelling from further afield. The staff at Bowerham Barracks had been working hard day and night for more than a week when the mobilisation order was actually received. Shortly afterwards the Proclamation was placarded on the walls of the barracks, at the Town Hall, police stations and other public places. The response was immediate and on 6 August large numbers of men arrived at the barracks, many from all over north-west England, some from even further afield. Here they were issued with their kit and quickly sent away by special trains to various destinations: some were sent to Plymouth, where the 3rd (Special Reserve) Battalion established its training base, and others were despatched to Dover where the 1st Battalion was based.

A small contingent of the people arriving in the town on 6 August included an escort from the 1st Battalion who travelled from Dover to Lancaster with their Regimental Colours, which were to be placed in the Regimental Chapel. Their arrival was not generally known and only a few people witnessed the handing over. Before receiving the Colours from Lieutenants Irving and Statter, the Vicar of Lancaster, Reverend J.U.N. Bardsley, said that he had received a letter from Lieutenant Colonel Dykes, the Commanding Officer of the 1st Battalion, stating that the battalion had been ordered to mobilise for active service, and he was sending the Colours to the Depot, in order to be placed in the Chapel. Lieutenant Colonel Dykes wrote:

I know that you will gladly accept this responsibility until we can return to claim them, and I also know that we shall have the prayers of yourself and your congregation that the Regiment may maintain its proud traditions and new honours to its Colours in the performance of whatever duty it may be called upon to undertake.

The vicar received the Colours and placed them on opposite sides of the altar, along with the Colours of the 5th Battalion which had been deposited the previous day. Shaking hands with the colour-bearers, the vicar said: 'I wish you God's blessing, and that you may return safe and sound.' Today, the Memorial Chapel displays one of the most complete collections of Regimental Colours in the country.

The vicar's wish was not granted. As described in Chapter 4, the 1st Battalion was quickly moved to France where it immediately became caught up in desperate fighting as the British Expeditionary Force retreated from Mons. Less than a month after carrying the Colours, Charles Irving was severely wounded and captured on 26 August at Haucort, near Le Cateau – he spent the rest of the war in captivity. William Statter was wounded a few days later at Courrois on 8 September – he recovered, was transferred to the Royal Flying Corps in January 1916, and survived the war. Lieutenant Colonel Dykes was less fortunate – a veteran of the South African War of 1899–1902, he was killed in the same action that led to Irving's capture.

The 5th Battalion

Like all Territorial Force battalions, the 5th Battalion was designated for a Home Defence role and the men could not be ordered overseas. They could, however, volunteer for Imperial Service which they did, reportedly every single man. With this in mind, the battalion was released of its duties in Barrow-in-Furness and returned to Lancaster on 12 August 1914. They urgently needed a suitable place for accommodation so temporary barracks were

Interior view of 5th Battalion soldiers billeted at the former Wagon Works, Caton Road, Lancaster, 12/13/14 August 1914. (KOM)

Soldiers of the 5th Battalion, King's Own, march down Caton Road from the temporary barracks at the former wagon works to Lancaster Castle Railway Station, 14 August 1914. (KOM)

established in the old Lancaster Railway Carriage and Wagon Works on Caton Road, which had been empty since the works closed in 1908. After two days there, the 5th Battalion received their orders to move to Didcot, Oxfordshire where they would guard lines of communication, particularly the Great Western Railway. The battalion departed the Wagon Works and marched along Caton Road to Lancaster Castle Station (now Lancaster station) for their transport to the south. The first train load left at 1.05 p.m. amidst cheers from the spectators, with the second departing thirty-five minutes later. Large numbers of people gathered on the line side south of Lancaster Castle Station, and cheered the departing officers and men. On 15 August the 5th Battalion arrived in Didcot which was to be their main base and detachments were sent along the Great Western Railway line in order to guard bridges and other important points.

The military's thirst for men was evident from the outset. Before the battalion departed, extensive efforts had been made to recruit more men to it and other units. On 7 August as many as 200 men were sworn in and equipped as members of the Territorial Battalion. Even so, when the battalion arrived at Didcot, an assessment took place of the 938 men who had volunteered for overseas service and it was discovered that between 200 and 300 of them were either unfit, too young, or simply changed their mind about overseas active service. As a result, in early September an appeal was sent to Lancaster for recruits to come forward to join the 5th Battalion. Recruiting meetings were held in both Lancaster and Morecambe with Major Bates, the battalion's second-in-command, and Captain Seward addressing those present. They were frequently supported by others: for example, at a meeting at Waring and Gillows' works they were joined on the platform by Mr S.J. Waring, one of the company directors.

The Commanding Officer of the 5th Battalion, Lord Richard Cavendish, spoke at a meeting in the Central School at Morecambe in early September 1914. He told the audience that Britain was fighting 'to fulfil a solemn obligation to protect the weak' (a reference to the fact that the country had gone to war

Group of 5th Battalion, King's Own, soldiers with some local people at Goring-on-Thames, when guarding the Great Western Railway mainline between Didcot and Reading against enemy attacks, 8 September 1914. (KOM)

Sergeant George Snowden and other members of the 5th Battalion, King's Own, at Green Lane Bridge, when guarding the Great Western Railway, c. September 1914. (KOM)

in response to the German invasion of Belgium). He went on to ask the audience whether any man 'capable of bearing arms … could calmly acknowledge that he was doing nothing to meet his country's need'. His wife, Lady Cavendish, also addressed the meeting, calling on the women of Morecambe and Lancaster to encourage their sons and brothers to enlist.

Lord Cavendish further explained that the War Office had sent down instructions that further battalions could be raised

for home defence as the 5th Battalion would be sent to serve overseas. In the early days of September hundreds of men came forward to join what became known as the Lancaster Pals and Morecambe Pals. From the volunteers, 200 men were selected to leave Lancaster on Sunday 6 September to journey to Didcot to begin their military training. This group of men were christened the 'Gallant 200' by the local press. They had had no previous military training. They were put through their paces with a regular programme which included all forms of military drill but also domestic duties such as the daily potato-peeling duty.

The recruiting drive continued throughout September 1914, with mixed results. At one meeting in Lancaster, Herbert Lushington Storey expressed disappointment that the hall was not more crowded. He told the audience that he feared there was too much popular ignorance of 'the object and meaning of the war', and described how in one recent visit to a factory in Manchester he discovered that only 200 out of the 5,000 workers had enlisted. He was confident that the people of Lancaster 'knew better, because they were always more or less in touch with

The motor lorry acquired by the 5th Battalion, King's Own, from Barrow Corporation in August 1914, was taken with the battalion to Didcot and used by the battalion to obtain supplies. Regimental Quartermaster Sergeant Woodcock is sitting in the cab: he was a long-time member of the 5th Battalion and Volunteers and had seen active service in the South African War 1899–1902. (KOM)

23

1ˢᵗ Volunteer Battalion, King's Own Royal Lancaster Regiment, Lieutenant Colonel Lord Richard Cavendish, Commanding Officer, alongside his motorcycle, c. 1907. (KOM)

the military'. He ended his speech by telling the audience that 'if he were a young man he would not be long in coming forward'. Lord Cavendish addressed the same meeting, using similar language, describing it as the 'solemn and bounden duty' of every man who could bear arms to come forward. He also appealed to local patriotism, describing the enthusiastic response of the men of Morecambe and Fleetwood to the call to join up. The Mayor

followed by calling on men in the audience to volunteer. The local press reports suggest that the response was less impressive than the speakers hoped. Just a few men came forward and only 'after some delay'.

Recruitment for the 5th Battalion continued into October resulting in the 5th (Reserve) Battalion being established to allow training to be undertaken in the local area. This battalion was eventually to become the 2nd/5th Battalion of the King's Own, with the original 5th Battalion being re-designated as the 1st/5th.

The 2nd/5th Battalion trained many men over the following months, some of whom were sent overseas to join the 1st/5th Battalion on the Western Front. Eventually, in February 1917, the entire battalion left for active service in France and Belgium.

New volunteers for the 5th Battalion, King's Own, parade from the Priory Church, Lancaster, on 6 September 1914. Christened the 'Gallant 200', they would depart for Didcot later that same day to begin their military training. (KOM)

One of the 5th Battalion's first casualties was Lance Corporal Arthur Gordon who was knocked down by a train near Faringdon, Oxfordshire. He was reported as being from Morecambe's West End but probably had no local family as he is buried in St. Mary's Churchyard, Uffington.

25

Soldiers of the 5th Battalion, King's Own, undergo military training at Didcot, September 1914. (KOM)

Soldiers of the 5th Battalion, King's Own, outside the former Corn Exchange at Didcot involved in the daily potato 'bashing' or peeling duty. (KOM)

Recruiting Kitchener's Army

Predicting the need for a mass army in a lengthy war, in August 1914 Lord Kitchener, the Secretary of State for War, made an appeal for 100,000 men to volunteer for War Service. This led to the creation of the 6th, 7th, 8th and 9th Battalions of the King's Own Royal Lancaster Regiment as 'war service' battalions. Recruiting for these new battalions, and indeed other units of the army, took place across the district, but the centre of operations was shared between the Old Town Hall in Market Square and at Bowerham Barracks. Men attested for military service and underwent their medical examinations at the Old Town Hall. Major Burdoch, the recruiting officer, made an appeal in mid-August to local owners of motor cars to loan them for the purpose of bringing in recruits from the country districts. Many were quick to respond and cars in the charge of military men were seen all across the region. Bowerham Barracks was busy with the arrival of new recruits, who were arriving from all parts of Lancashire, a far larger county then than it is today. Men would be equipped with what was available and then despatched to the quickly-established training camps in the South of England. A shortage of uniforms rapidly

Soldiers of the newly-formed 8th (Service) Battalion, King's Own, wearing blue uniforms, due to shortage of khaki material, but each also wore a small lapel badge which had '8 KORL' on it. (KOM)

became an issue and one photo shows men of the 8th Battalion wearing a blue uniform rather than the khaki, the material clearly in short supply, and with a shortage of King's Own cap badges, which features the Lion of England, the men wore a small badge on their lapel marked with '8 KORL'.

The numbers of men in the 5th (Reserve) Battalion continued to grow, although by mid-September at least 180 men were still required to complete the battalion. Lancaster had provided 320 men, Fleetwood and district 140 and Morecambe 120. The men were in the charge of Captain Keen, who was assisted by two officers and three non-commissioned officers. A full programme of training of drill, except with arms, was carried out, and the men coped well with all that they were doing, including some long route marches. Additional officers were required and it was expected that these would be made up from the ranks. A shortage of uniforms meant that the men of the 5th (Reserve) Battalion had to train in their civilian clothes. Their service in the Colours was marked with a blue and orange silk ribbon worn on their shoulder.

An open-air recruiting meeting in Market Square on Wednesday 23 September pressed home the need for 200 more

New volunteers to the 5th Battalion, King's Own, on parade at Giant Axe Field, who had come forward following the appeal for 200 volunteers from the battalion in Didcot, September 1914. (KOM)

THE 5th K.O. PALS COY d/s

Silk shoulder ribbon of the King's Own Regiment's colours, blue and orange, worn by the volunteers of the 5th (Reserve) Battalion, King's Own, prior to the arrival of their uniforms. (KOM)

men to volunteer. 'Will you do it?' asked Captain Keen, as the Mayor presided over the large gathering. Captain Keen pointed out that the 5th Battalion could not go to the front until the home defence battalion was formed. Chief Constable Harriss also addressed the gathering, stating that he had never thought he would become a recruiting sergeant because he was a man of peace and detested war. However, he had read the articles in the newspaper and raised the real danger of the fear of invasion. 'Let's have the 200 men needed' he concluded, the National Anthem was sung, and as the meeting ended, some young men accompanied the officers to the recruiting station.

As the nights lengthened, the reserve battalion departed Lancaster at the start of November and moved to Blackpool where they continued their training. They then moved to Kent where they

The silk ribbons worn by men of the 5th (Reserve) Battalion were made by the ladies of Lancaster. The regimental colours of royal blue and orange date back to the regiment's support of William of Orange when he landed at Torbay in 1688 (see picture above).

took over the billets vacated by the 1st/5th Battalion when they departed for the Western Front on Valentine's Day 1915.

Bowerham Barracks

During the first month of the war, staff at Bowerham Barracks dealt with more than 2,000 recruits, sent to Lancaster from as far away as Manchester and even London. These men were equipped and then sent on to the new Kitchener battalions. The barracks was forced to accommodate many more men than it was designed for, sometimes as many as five times the number. Some of the men who arrived were in an almost destitute condition, and some local women had a whip round for clothing to tide them over before they could be issued with service clothing. Locations all over town emphasised their presence: marquees at Bowerham Council School and in the barrack fields were utilised for accommodation; the YMCA provided recreation for the men in their rooms on King Street; and Herbert Lushington Storey

Members of the 5th (Reserve) Battalion, King's Own, outside the YMCA on King Street, Lancaster. The YMCA also established a marquee at Bowerham Barracks shortly after the start of the war. (KOM)

provided a marquee at Bowerham Barracks, which was equipped with materials and reading matter for the use of the troops. On 17 September 1,100 recruits left Bowerham Barracks for Seaford, Sussex, where they were to form the King's Own's new 8th Battalion.

By the end of September, as many as 7,000 men had passed through the Depot at Bowerham. 1,100 reservists were equipped and sent away in the first four days of mobilisation. Three full battalions of the Kitchener Army had been sent out and orders had been received to fit out another 2,000 men. Over fifty reservists from Canada and the Colonies had rejoined the Colours. And the war had barely begun.

Conclusions

The logistics of war were only to become more challenging as the war continued. The presence of the King's Own was to have a huge effect on Lancaster's experience of the war. Its presence must have inspired many of the town's young men to join up and, as we shall see, the experiences of its battalions, particularly the 1st/5th, was to have major impacts on the town, particularly when these units were involved in actions that led to large numbers of casualties.

2

ATTITUDES TO THE WAR

The outbreak of war

It is often assumed that the people of Britain responded with universal enthusiasm to the country's entry into the First World War on 4 August 1914. King George and Queen Mary were loudly cheered when they appeared on the balcony at the front of Buckingham Palace, a few hours after a state of war had been declared between Britain and Germany. The *Daily News* reported how crowds surged through Westminster and Charing Cross singing patriotic songs and waving flags. It would be wrong, though, to assume that the war was welcomed by everyone. The King himself had noted in his diary a few days earlier that many people were against any British involvement in a European conflict. In some northern cities, like Huddersfield and Leeds, there were many voices arguing that the industrial workers who filled the mills and factories had little stake in the conflict. Nor was everyone convinced that the war would be over by Christmas. The publication of countless invasion-scare books and articles over the previous twenty years, describing how modern warfare was likely to be far more brutal than anything previously

Food shortages followed the declaration of war, more because farmers, suppliers and shop keepers were holding back stock and individuals were panic buying. The production of food was affected by the number of young men joining the military and, from 1917, the German policy of unrestricted submarine warfare.

A food queue at Brock Street outside Speight's, listed in Bulmer's Directory of Lancaster and District as a 'confectioner and fruiterer'. (LCM)

known, meant that the news of war was often met with apprehension as much as jingoism.

The outbreak of war in Lancaster was met less with elaborate displays of patriotism and more with a sober determination to face whatever lay ahead. The *Lancaster Observer and Morecambe Chronicle* (hereafter *Lancaster Observer*) ran an article warning that 'immense carnage is coming, and commercial and trade desolations'. The paper's first edition after the declaration of war noted that 'popular demonstrations' in the town had shown 'a subdued character'. It also noted that the departure of the first wave of local territorial forces 'was marked by no such excitement as was witnessed fourteen years ago' (during the Boer War). The cautious mood was heightened by several warnings from local businessmen that Lancaster's factories might have to close if it proved impossible to import cotton and other vital raw materials. Local shoppers rushed to buy staple foodstuffs, alarmed at rumours of shortages, with a resulting rise in the price of goods including butter and sugar. The cancellation of summer fetes and holiday railway excursions added to the sense of crisis.

In the days that followed the outbreak of war, the people of Lancaster volunteered in large numbers for service in the local

The first of a series of weekly sales of local farm produce raised £8 13s 2d for the Mayor of Lancaster's Relief Fund. The first sale, held outside the Town Hall, in November 1914 included two turkeys, a prize-winning leek and a 40lb cheese. (LCM)

hospital, in expectation of the arrival of casualties. The Town Council announced the establishment of a Distress Committee to raise funds for the dependents of those who volunteered to fight, as well as the families of workers expected to lose their jobs. The Mayor, Councillor William Briggs, was typical of many of Lancaster's dignitaries in calling for practical measures to help the town cope with the disruption of war. His wife Mary established twice-weekly sewing parties for local women to produce gloves and blankets for the troops. Lord Ashton made a large donation to help those facing poverty. The local press continued to warn that 'the country must be prepared for a long and arduous struggle'. By the third week of August, the *Lancaster Observer* noted that there was 'a wonderful calmness' in the town, as local people began to face the war with determination rather than frenzied nationalism.

The sober tone was reinforced by local clergy and ministers of religion. The main denominations in Britain all moved quickly to express support for the war, although some opposition was heard among the Primitive Methodists and Baptists, whilst members of the Society of Friends generally remained true to their long tradition of pacifism. The tone of the sermons preached in the early weeks of the war was, though, once again cautious and restrained. Although some Anglican clergy across Britain used their pulpit to encourage men to enlist in the forces, the Vicar of Lancaster was more measured, telling his congregation that although war was evil it was not a crime:

> It was no use whinging about war, and trying to run away from it ... All sensible people shrink from war, just as they shrink from the surgeon's knife. But when disease came, and they were faced with an operation, it was their duty to accept it with resignation as if it was coming from God.

Mayor Briggs and his wife Mary Alice, née Stanton, on the steps of Lancaster Town Hall, both wearing chains of office. The photograph was taken on 19 October 1919, at the return of the cadre of the 1st/5th Battalion, King's Own, which had spent time in Ireland after it had left Belgium in the summer of 1919. (KOM)

Quiet resignation rather than celebration continued to characterise the reaction of many residents of Lancaster during the weeks that followed. The sewing parties organised by the Mayoress were devoid of 'frivolity or gossip'. And while there was strong support for soldiers heading off for service, the ceremonies were still largely devoid of jingoism, and 'the cheering was subdued but nonetheless hearty'.

Recruitment and conscription

Recruiting Handbill of the 1st/5th Battalion, King's Own Royal Lancaster Regiment, in 1915.

The mood of subdued patriotism, characterised by a focus on the kind of practical measures needed to respond to the challenges of war, was not perhaps surprising in a town with a large military presence and residents used to the challenge of hard work in the local mills and factories. It was not, though, calculated to foster the kind of exuberant sentiment needed to encourage the young men of Lancaster and the surrounding towns and villages to enlist. The British army in 1914 was a volunteer force, far smaller than its continental counterparts, and remained so even following the mobilisation of the territorial reserves during the first weeks of the war. Lord Kitchener, who became Secretary of State for War the day after war was declared, quickly put in motion a recruiting campaign intended to attract a large number of volunteers to bolster Britain's military forces. Nearly half a million men responded by the end of September, a huge number, but

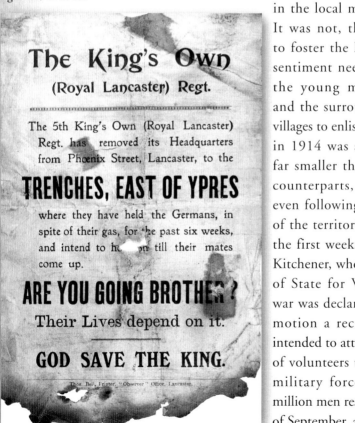

The King's Own
(Royal Lancaster) Regt.

The 5th King's Own (Royal Lancaster) Regt. has removed its Headquarters from Phœnix Street, Lancaster, to the

TRENCHES, EAST OF YPRES

where they have held the Germans, in spite of their gas, for the past six weeks, and intend to h.. on till their mates come up.

ARE YOU GOING BROTHER?

Their Lives depend on it.

GOD SAVE THE KING.

Thos. Bell, Printer, "Observer" Office, Lancaster.

still far less than was needed as it became clear that the small British Expeditionary Force already in France would be utterly inadequate for the battles that lay ahead. The recruiting campaign continued over the following months, complete with posters designed to appeal to the patriotic instincts of potential volunteers and play on their fears of being thought a coward by their friends and family.

The local papers in Lancaster proudly reported on the gallantry of the men who served in the King's Own. In April 1918 the *Lancaster Observer* described how one Pte R. Corbett took command of his platoon when all the officers and NCOs were killed in action, successfully continuing the attack on a German trench mortar.

Both the *Lancaster Observer* and *Lancaster Guardian* regularly printed columns during the early months of the year proudly noting that the town was providing more than its fair share of recruits. The presence of the King's Own Royal Lancaster Regiment undoubtedly helped to fuel local patriotism. The two papers also took a lead in criticising young 'shirkers' who refused to join up, and who did 'not seem to realize that the call is to them'. Both papers reflected the prevailing sense that the justice of Britain's cause was unquestionable. A similar tone prevailed at the large recruitment meetings held in Lancaster and Morecambe, as part of Lord Kitchener's drive to attract large numbers of volunteers, where local dignitaries and army officers called for men to come forward and join the forces. Some local women wanted to do even more. 'Margherita' wrote to the *Lancaster Observer* calling on the women of north Lancashire to learn to use weapons effectively, so they could, if necessary, take part in defending their homeland, should the Germans invade Britain.

Recruitment seemed to have been particularly problematic in the rural areas around Lancaster, in part because small family farms would struggle to survive with the loss of even one or two men, unlike the large factories of Lancaster. Accusations that the villages stretched along the Lune Valley were not 'doing their bit' predictably infuriated some local people. One resident from the village of Wray acknowledged that there were 'shirkers' there, but added that some locals had already joined up, while the ladies were 'knitting furiously' and the older men were volunteering as Special Constables.

Herbert Lushington Storey (in the uniform of Deputy Lieutenant of Lancashire (High Sheriff) in 1904). (LCM)

Recruitment drives continued right down to the introduction of conscription early in 1916. The speeches at recruiting meetings, along with articles in local newspapers, provided some of the most robust defences of Britain's role in the war against the Central Powers. By the spring of 1915, there was growing concern that recruitment was running at such a level that the loss of workers from Lancaster's biggest factories might force them to shut down altogether. Lord Ashton raised the issue at length with the War Office, leading to suggestions in some quarters that the town's business leaders were not suffi-ciently patriotic, a charge that was unfair and rejected locally. Both Herbert Lushington Storey and the Lancaster MP Norval Helme followed Lord Ashton in warning about the danger of recruiting disproportionately from the biggest factories. All three men forcefully argued that there was nothing unpatriotic about wanting to keep Lancaster's economy prosperous, and its people employed, working in factories that played an important role in the war effort.

The local newspapers printed extensive commentary about the progress of the war, giving particular attention to the activi-ties of the various battalions of the King's Own. The recruiting drives that took place throughout 1915 continued to build on the town's pride in its strong military connections. In early June, Major J.H. Bates of the 1st/5th Battalion, who had been invalided home from the Second Battle of Ypres and whose son had been killed there, addressed a large recruiting meeting with the rousing call 'Are you going brother?'. He spoke vividly of the heavy losses among local Lancaster men at the Front, telling his audience their 'memory would never die as long as we live'. Bates called on mothers to encourage their sons to join up, describing how hundreds of young Belgian girls had to 'hang their heads in shame as a result of the vile conduct of the fiends the Allies were fighting'. Later that day, bands marched through Lancaster's Market Square playing martial music, and local dignitaries gave rousing speeches calling for recruits. A telegram was read out from Lord Derby, who headed the national recruiting campaign, noting that 'We want all we can get to fill again the ranks of Lord Richard Cavendish's splendid battalion.' The local MP called on the young men of Lancaster to join up and 'bring about a glorious victory' as soon as possible. The streets of the town resounded in the early summer evening with a blend of music and speeches, which together created a celebration of the rightness of Britain's cause, and encouraged those present to reflect on what they could do to work for their country's victory.

The pressure on the young men of Lancaster to volunteer became still stronger in the final months of 1915, at a time when

James Edgar Leach VC at Lancaster Town Hall, flanked by the Mayor and Mayoress (seated). (LCM KOM)

the prospect of conscription was becoming more real, given the scale of the losses on the Western Front and at Gallipoli. In August the *Lancaster Observer* listed twelve excuses commonly given by 'shirkers' for not joining up ('the saddest form of unmanliness' it remarked). The paper noted caustically that some men believed their 'position was too good to give up' whilst others believed that army pay was 'totally insufficient'. Other 'excuses' – at least to modern eyes – seem less self-centred ('I believe in religion'; 'the dependants' allowance will not properly maintain my relatives').

In September Lord Derby visited Lancaster, where he called for more men from the countryside to join up, while Herbert Storey told the same meeting that he was now in favour of conscription. Both local papers supported the introduction of the so-called Derby Scheme a few weeks later, which required men who were less than 41 years old, and not in a protected occupation, to declare whether they were prepared to fight. In Lancaster – as elsewhere across Britain – canvassers visited the homes of thousands of local men to encourage them to register (more than 30,000 men in Lancaster, Morecambe and the surrounding area received such calls). The King's Own was by now only recruiting a fraction of the men it needed, a pattern that was repeated up and down the country, with the result that the Military Service Act introducing conscription was finally passed in January 1916. In Lancaster a large number of men rushed to enlist voluntarily, while they still had the opportunity, perhaps mindful that by volunteering they would avoid the charge of refusing to serve their country until they had no choice.

The introduction of conscription meant an end to the big recruiting rallies and some of the most stirring rhetoric of 1914 and 1915. Chapter 6 shows how attention instead began to focus more on the supposed lack of courage of the men who sought exemption from military service. In any case the carnage on the Western Front and elsewhere meant that from the very start of the war the language of patriotism had to acknowledge the realities of pain and loss. The sheer scale of human misery, which was only too obvious in a place like Lancaster, which suffered so many casualties (see Chapter 5), became part of a rhetoric that accepted sacrifice as an integral part of Britain's experience of war. The town was certainly happy to welcome heroes like Lieutenant James Leach of the Manchester Regiment, born in Bowerham Barracks, who won the Victoria Cross for his heroism when fighting near in northern France in October 1914 (see Chapter 8). But it was also important for the anxious and bereaved to find solace in the belief that loved ones were fighting and dying heroically for a good cause.

Letters home

Soldiers' letters from the Front played an important role in helping the people of Lancaster understand the lives of their friends and relatives on the battlefield. Censorship meant that some details were withheld, either by the men themselves, or by the officers responsible for checking their correspondence. Even so, while relatives were spared some of the more brutal details of life in and behind the trenches, the letters often gave a good insight into the challenges of modern warfare. Both the *Lancaster*

Observer and the *Lancaster Guardian* published hundreds of extracts from them during the years between 1914 and 1918. The picture painted by the letters reproduced in the two newspapers' columns was, for the most part, one of quiet determination and confidence about the justice of Britain's cause. Such sentiment – as in Lancaster itself – was probably more representative than the extravagant rhetoric of the recruiting rallies of 1914 and 1915.

A few extracts from some letters sent home by soldiers to their families reveals how many of the men wanted to describe their experiences while sheltering their relatives from the full horrors of combat. In a letter written some time after Christmas 1914, Private Richard Gaughan from Bare thanked his friends and family for a package of chocolates and mince pies, which made a refreshing change from 'bully beef and biscuits'. With these pleasantries out of the way, he went on to describe how the landscape where he was fighting had been 'blown to atoms', while 'the whiz of bullets and the crash of shells makes you realise what a terrible thing war is'. Other soldiers were equally frank about the conditions under which they struggled. In May 1915, a soldier from Lancaster wrote home describing the scenes as his unit advanced out of the trenches, 'the beautiful spring day' made 'hideous' by the shells falling around him. He was surprised that he 'felt no fear', even when hit by shrapnel, after which he was taken to a field-station from where he was writing. In the same month, the *Lancaster Observer* printed a letter from an officer in the 1st/5th Battalion, King's Own, describing how his men had recently been 'badly mauled' at the Second Battle of Ypres. Another letter-writer vividly told what it was like to be gassed.

This combination of honesty and bravery remained the hallmark of many soldiers' letters home over the months and years that followed. Relatives sent copies of the correspondence to the newspapers, which were happy to print material that acknowledged the difficult conditions of war, while at the same time capturing the determination and bravery of the troops. Many letters were remarkably positive about the German forces they faced, praising their military skill, and avoiding some of the more hostile language that routinely appeared in the press back in Britain. Soldiers seldom dwelt at length on the rights and wrongs of the war, at least beyond a perfunctory expression of belief that they were fighting for a good cause. The Lancaster newspapers sometimes sought to create a more positive tone in their columns by printing news of awards for valour made to men from Lancaster, and soldiers belonging to the King's Own, describing the acts for which they had been commended. They also carried details of men who had been wounded, or gone missing, and were occasionally able to carry more pleasant stories of how soldiers feared dead had been found alive and taken to hospital. More common, though, were reports of men who had died, many of which are summarised or reproduced on the *Reveille* website.

Relatives and friends of soldiers killed on the battlefield were often desperate for news of how their loved-ones had died. The commanding officers and chaplains were equally determined not to be too graphic in their accounts. The brutal character of life and death on the battlefield was almost impossible to comprehend for those fortunate enough not to experience it first-hand. The letters sent to bereaved relatives that were published in the Lancaster press – and in other newspapers up and down Britain – almost invariably paid homage to the bravery of the dead man and his popularity among his colleagues. They were usually economical in providing details about how they died.

A few examples reveal the character of many of the letters giving news of the death of a son or brother or husband. In May 1915, the widow of Private Thomas Towers received a letter from his Commanding Officer, telling her that he had been shot in the head and died later at an ambulance station. In the same month, the mother of Private Victor Keyworth from Bolton le Moors received a letter from his corporal, who came from Lancaster, describing how her son had been shot in the mouth, and before dying had asked that his friends write to her to offer his good-byes. A few months later, the widow of Private Alfred Bewes of the 2nd Battalion, King's Own, received a letter describing how her husband had been hit by shell fragments and died shortly afterwards: 'He died a soldier's death.' Similar letters flooded

Letter-writing in the First World War

With separation came letter-writing, fostered by boredom, and the yearning for loved ones and news of home or abroad. To give a sense of the scale of the postal operation of the war, we need only to look at some statistics. At its peak, 12.5 million letters and a million parcels left the purpose-built sorting depot at Regent's Park every week, while letters back were collected from the men from field post offices across the Front. Over the course of the war, the British Army Postal Service delivered around 2 billion letters. Since the Boer War, the British Army had been well aware of the importance of post to maintaining morale, but the logistics of the operation were challenged by the scale of operations, and the importance of maintaining censorship to avoid information falling into the wrong hands.

Correspondence was read in a number of contrasting ways – in snatched moments of privacy and stored safe close to the body, shared more openly with relatives, friends or comrades to permit snippets of news to be collated and discussed, and more openly still in the local press, as shown in this chapter. Such letters encourage us not to over-emphasise the gulf of experi-ence between the home and the battlefront, even if prose could never convey all the dimensions of experience. Letters also played a significant part in fostering rumours between the fronts: a report into the morals of the Women's Auxiliary Army Corps on the Western Front concluded, for example, that its poor reputation was the consequence of rumours started in letters home-fuelled by the 'jealousy and hostility' of men 'dislodged from non-combatant tasks in the bases' by the arrival of the women.

One of the strangest experiences of war must have been receiving letters from the dead: it took at least two days for post between the Western Front and Great Britain. In Gallipoli, more unopened letters whose intended recipients had been killed in action had to be sent back from the front than letters going forward. The General Post Office did seek to ensure that returned letters did not arrive before informing the next of kin of the death. In a letter to her brother, Vera Brittain described witnessing when her deceased

A MOTHER'S STRANGE EXPERIENCE.

Pte. Albert Sandham, whose parents live in Mill-street, sent word on Sunday morning that Pte. Frederick Lupton, aged 21, one of the family of ten surviving children of Mr. and Mrs. Jas. Lupton, of 34, Garnet-street, had been killed in action. He had been in the battalion four years, and was attending what would have been his last camp when the order to mobilise was issued. Lupton was a National school boy, and was employed at Lune Works. His elder brother is serving with the local artillery at Westerham.

Mrs. Lupton, who is distraught with grief at her bereavement, had a curious experience on Wednesday evening of last week. She was preparing to go to bed when, she says, she distinctly heard her son call out "Mother" three times. The effect on her was most disconcerting, but it prepared her somewhat for the blow that Sunday brought.

In his letter Sandham says the battalion is now only 300 strong. "We have done our share of duty," he adds, "but still we are quite happy among it all."

The 'strange experience' of hearing Pte Frederick Lupton (Killed in Action) from beyond the grave, as reported in the Lancaster Observer, *14 May 1915. (MJH)*

fiancé's returned kit was received by his mother: 'These were his clothes - the clothes in which he came home from the front last time. Everything was damp and worn and simply caked with mud … We discovered that the bullet was an expanding one. The hole where it went in in front – well below where the belt would have been, just below the right-hand bottom pocket of the tunic - was almost microscopic, but at the back, almost exactly where his back bone would have been, there was quite a large rent.' On the other hand, parcels received at the front bringing supplies from home could make all the difference to morale, offering an opportunity, for example, to share a taste of home with comrades - if the rats had not got there first.

9 Dale St.
Lancaster.
14.9.016.

Mrs Outram
Newlands Hall.

Dear Madam,
Many thanks for your kind letter of sympathy in my sad loss, and also of my son Fred.
I got a letter from a friend of my son's, to say that he was seriously wounded in the head, on the 1st of August and was taken to a dressing station. Several of my friends have tried to get further information for me, but have not been successful, until Capt: Raper wrote and he got a letter back from Capt: Eavis saying he was in hospital, and alive when his letter left the front.
I then received a letter from the record office saying he was wounded but place not stated. I have not heard anything since. I am very anxious about him.
I should be glad if

This letter from Jane Monks, mother of Corporal F.V. Monks, of the King's Own, describes receiving multiple letters reporting contradictory news of her son. Between the lines, we can read both desperation and hope.

back to Lancaster throughout the war years, many printed in the *Lancaster Observer* and *Lancaster Guardian*, telling how men had 'been killed instantly', or lived just long enough to send fond farewells to their loved ones.

It was usually impossible to know the precise circumstances of an individual soldier's death. Some were lucky enough to die quickly from a bullet wound to the head or a direct hit from a shell, but many more died slow and agonising deaths. The Wesleyan Methodist chaplain Robert Wearmouth, who worked for long periods of time in field-hospitals in northern France, later recalled how when he wrote to the bereaved he carefully spared them the details about how their loved ones died. Nor was he alone. Lots of those who tended the wounded recalled the horrors of infected wounds, gangrene, maggots, gas burns and amputations. The heroism of the men condemned to such awful fates was not in any way reduced by the agonies they suffered. But the conventions of the letters home to the bereaved,

your son would be
able to send me any
news of him.
There are all kinds of
reports, only this week
I heard he was killed.
I think I ought to
know something more
definate from the war
office. I enclose his full
name and number, so
that your son may
recognise if he was
his servant. again
thanking you for your
kind inquiries I remain.
  Yours sincerely.
    Jane. Monks.

Copl: E. V. Monks
Ste. 5th Kings Own
N⁰. 2153.

wounded on the
14th august.

Ko 2490/123

whether from commanding officers and chaplains, or simply
from friends, required a language of dignity and selflessness that
was in many cases illusory. The rhetoric of approval – the use
of a language that emphasised the justice of Britain's cause and
the heroism of its soldiers – placed an emphasis on bravery and
sacrifice rather than the harsh realities of mechanised slaughter.
The bereaved of Lancaster, like every town and village up and
down Britain, preferred to imagine their loved ones lying whole
in a quiet grave, rather than as a mangled and incomplete body
buried hastily with others in the shallow earth. Yet that was the
fate of many who died in the First World War.

The obituaries of dead soldiers in the Lancaster papers were
typically written in a way that emphasised both their service to
their country and their close ties to their home town. When the
death of Captain Charles Hinton from Scotforth was reported
in May 1918, the *Lancaster Observer* gave a long account of the
career of 'a gallant soldier and a brave Englishman'. Nor was it

only officers who received such attention (although their obituaries were generally longer). The same edition of the *Lancaster Observer* reported the death of Private George Townley from Skerton, describing his time in Lancaster at Waring and Gillow, as well as giving details of the service record of his brother. The paper also reported the deaths of several other Lancaster men during the previous week, and gave details of the wounded, as well as providing information about those taken prisoner. The language used in these reports was typically factual rather than hyperbolic. The men who had lost their lives for their country were praised for fulfilling their duty as patriotic Englishmen. The tone echoed the language in which the First World War was generally discussed in Lancaster and its environs: as a conflict forced upon Britain, to which its people had to respond, rather than as an occasion for great outpourings of jingoism and nationalism. In the final years of the war, in particular, quiet patriotism and determination to work for victory were the order of the day for many in Lancaster.

Families of men at the Front often found it hard to get definite news of their loved ones. The wife of Harry Winder, who lived at 12 St Leonard's Gate, only knew for certain that her husband was dead when another Lancaster soldier wrote to say that Winder had been killed with ten other men by a German shell: 'This big battle is terrible and takes the nerves out of a chap.'

Conclusions

The civic leaders of Lancaster – its councillors, businessmen, newspaper editors and ministers of religion – were unanimous in 1914 that Britain was fighting for a good cause and they believed that their town should play its full part in the struggle. They also encouraged its young (and not so young) men to fight. They played their part in helping Lancaster become a major centre for the manufacture of munitions. The leading civic figures in the town sometimes disagreed on matters of detail, such as balancing the needs of the local economy and the needs of recruitment, but they were wholeheartedly committed to the war effort. Yet the language they used in support of the war in Lancaster was marked as much by quiet talk of duty as it was by nationalist excess. The rhetoric of the recruiting campaigns was inspired by an instrumental need to encourage men to enlist – just as the accusation of cowardice was meant to shame them into the army – but it would be wrong to imagine that talk of 'shirkers' and 'huns' and 'heroes' was the only language in which war was discussed.

It is always easier to peer into the minds of businessmen and newspaper editors than it is into the minds of ordinary people. Yet all the evidence suggests that the people of Lancaster were overwhelmingly in support of the war, 'doing their bit', while accepting its agonies either with stoicism or private anguish. They took pride in the sons and brothers and husbands who went to fight. They believed that their loved ones fought for a good cause. And although they were on occasion ready to use or respond to the language of 'John Bull', more often they believed that war was a ghastly business, and something that had to be endured rather than enjoyed.

3

THE WAR AT HOME

News of the war

In Lancaster, the gulf between the battlefront and the home front was never wide. As the *Lancaster Guardian* pointed out, 'as a garrison town Lancaster has been in close touch with the war from its commencement.' Throughout the war, the newspapers were full of news from the battlefront, not just official communiques but details from letters submitted by the families of soldiers. The first inkling that the 1st/5th Battalion of the King's Own Royal Lancaster Regiment was at Ypres shortly after it had arrived in France, for example, came from the *Lancaster Guardian* of 10 April 1915, when it was reported that 'Several letters received from the men of the 5th King's Own Royal Lancaster Regiment refer to the fact that they have this week arrived at a famous town, which has loomed largely in the fighting of the western front.' A bookseller on New Street, Mr G.S. West, had two sons, Jack and Bert serving in the 'Pals'. On 10 April 1915, the *Lancaster Guardian* reported Mr West had received a batch of picture post-cards of Ypres from Bert, showing the shocking impact of the bombardment on the city. The losses during the Second Battle of Ypres (see chapters 4 and 5), when 121 Lancastrians died in six weeks in April and May 1915, led to a period when every news-paper edition brought home with 'greater intensity the terrible nature of the hostilities and appalling sacrifice of life involved'. As described in Chapter 2, these letters and reports did not lack graphic descriptions of the experience of warfare.

Newspapers were not the only media to offer coverage of the war to civilians. The North West Film Archive holds footage that would have been eagerly watched in one of the town's four cinemas: indeed the footage was often deliberately shot to include as many faces as possible to encourage viewers seeking a glimpse of loved ones. In late summer 1914, Thomas Scholey shot footage of men drilling outside of the Winter Gardens in Morecambe: without uniforms, they sported blue and orange flashes on their sleeves to demarcate them from civilians (see Chapter 1). There is footage of the collection of blankets for the troops, of men leaving from Lancaster Castle station, waved off by Mayor William Briggs and local dignitaries, catching in celluloid their flag-waving commitment to the war effort. Indeed there was much discussion in the press about who was allowed on the platform. Later in the war, there was considerable disgruntlement expressed by families not being allowed to wave goodbye to their loved ones: the blame was laid with the military controlling the space with an eye only to military efficiency. Not all war films were local of course. The most famous film of the war is perhaps 'The Battle of the Somme' filmed by Geoffrey Malins and John McDowell. The directors had for the first time been given permission to film at the front. This film probably did most to elevate cinema from lower-class entertainment to a fitting pastime for all. This was footage which appeared to offer authentic images of the war and offer a sense of immediacy. In the autumn of 1916 over 20 million Britons – half the population – saw it. In Lancaster, 'The Battle of the Somme' screened at the Lancaster Palladium in Market Street, on 5, 6 and 7 October. The *Lancaster Guardian* reported 'record houses … Quite a number (of Lancastrians) recognised relations amongst the fighting men.'

Foreign 'aliens'

There are interesting further indicators of how the home front engaged with the war. James Hayes has convincingly argued that the treatment of 'aliens' in Lancaster and Morecambe shows how much the home front was affected by the war and the extent to which individuals sought to be part of the war effort in whatever ways available to them. Foreign aliens had to register and the press was full of court proceedings against individuals of numerous nationalities (not only enemy nations) who had contravened the regulations on registration and movement, including a Mrs Margaret Kniel who was arrested in September 1914 for failing to register that she was of foreign birth. Born in Austria-Hungary, she had been a resident in Heysham since 1898. Some aliens were brought into the town from areas deemed vulnerable such as Morecambe, Manchester or Barrow-in-Furness: in August 1914, for example, thirty-two aliens from Barrow arrived in an attempt to protect the port from subversive activities.

Lancaster was not immune to the anti-German feeling which erupted across the country. The shop windows of Frederick Kramer, a pork butcher, were targeted in May 1915, when the newspapers were full of the local losses at Ypres and the sinking of the *Lusitania*. Kramer was of German parentage, but a naturalised Briton who had lived in Lancaster for many years. Lance-Corporal Joseph William O'Brien, 2nd Battalion, King's Own, was charged with wilful damage, but the main criticism expressed at his court case was that the cost of the repairs would have to be borne by the town. The mayor suggested instead boycotting such establishments, hoping that: 'Lancaster people would have the common-sense not to follow such a foolish example, but behave in a law-abiding manner, and not damage property in this way. If they had any feeling against shops of this kind they need not deal with them, and then they would soon be closed.'

The aliens greeted most sympathetically were the Belgians, although even they could be detained and penalised for poor registration practices. The press covered arrivals of refugees, termed 'fugitives', and their subsequent

On outbreak of war, the first two Germans to fall foul of the entry requirements for aliens arrived on a vessel that landed at Glasson Dock. Out at sea, they knew nothing of the outbreak of war, but were arrested immediately for lack of appropriate paperwork and subsequently interned.

experiences; a refugee house was opened in Morecambe, and families and employers such as Williamson's took them in.

Civilian internment of enemy aliens had been adopted at a national level from August 1914, serving the dual purpose of removing potential threats and bolstering morale on the home front. As Panikos Panayi has shown, by September 1914, 10,500 German resident civilians had been interned in Britain. By the May of the following year, all male civilian enemy aliens of military age were to be interned – by 1917, over 79,000 men. The speed with which this policy was put into practice led to makeshift camps, one of which was located in Lancaster in the Wagon Works on Caton Road.

There is a fascinating account of the flight to England by a young Belgian refugee from Antwerp, Irma Daems, which was published in the *Chronicle* of Lancaster's Girls Grammar School, at which she had become a pupil.

After the 5th Battalion, King's Own, left its temporary billets in the Wagon Works in August 1914 (see Chapter 1), it was only a few days before contractors from Nottingham had moved in to make the site secure, adding barbed wire to the walls and generally making the place ready to take 'prisoners of war' or interned illegal aliens. On 20 August a company of the 3rd Battalion, Royal Welsh Fusiliers, arrived to take charge of the prisoners, the first of which arrived on the following Monday, conveyed by direct train to the works' sidings. In the first week 380 prisoners arrived, many of them German seamen whose boats had been in British ports when war was declared. By the middle of September the camp population had swelled to 1,700 with prisoners arriving from Manchester, Newcastle and Carlisle. Most prisoners were German or Austrian nationals and predominantly adult males, however some were detained with their families, including children. One of Caton Road's most prominent internees was the then circus performer Joseph Hubertus Pilates who developed his physical regime of 'Contrology' not least in response to the constraints of incarceration. There is an account of conditions in the camp provided in a prison diary by Willy Wolff, a German Jew from Böchingen in the Rhineland, who had been working at a cotton brokerage in Salford since 1912

An exterior view of the camp in the Wagon Works, Caton Road. Some of the confusions in local lore – placing Joseph Pilates in the Castle, for example, can partially be explained by the indiscriminate use of the term 'prisoner of war' which blurs the distinction between foreign service personnel captured in the field and interned aliens. (LCM)

and subsequently interned in Lancaster. He described his arrival in the camp in 1914:

> October 5. Brought to Lancaster (3 captive Germans; 3 Policemen); Lancaster camp – an old, very dirty wagon factory that already had been shuttered for ten years. The appearance of the thousand internees already there was deplorable. The ovens were terribly primitive – built by the internees themselves. Nearly all of the people slept on straw mattresses on the damp floor.

Wolff's account of the camp is confirmed in other sources. Famously, in his autobiography *Goodbye to All That,* Robert Graves described his experience as a Royal Welch Fusilier guarding the camp:

> I went off on detachment duty to a newly-formed internment camp for enemy aliens at Lancaster ... a dirty, draughty place, littered with old scrap metal and guarded by high barbed wire fences. About three thousand prisoners had already arrived there, and more and

more crowded in every day: seamen were arrested on German vessels … waiters from large hotels in the north …, commercial travellers and shopkeepers. The prisoners resented being interned, particularly family men who had lived at peace in England for many years. The one comfort that we could offer them was "you are safer inside than out". For anti-German feeling had begun to run high …

There was much contradictory discussion as to the living conditions in the camp which was cold, draughty and dirty as well as overcrowded. At the same time the internees could exercise certain freedoms, such as holding sports days, or celebrating the Emperor of Austria-Hungary's birthday on 18 August 1915 through singing patriotic songs and enjoying a Bavarian military band. Boredom could foster creativity: on 8 January 1915, Wolff mentions prisoners had started 'the art of bone cutting' – carving bones to pass the time – two are held by the King's Own Royal Regiment Museum, and the Lancaster City Museum collection also holds examples of such pastimes. The prisoners' visibility could sometimes provoke local hostility, for example, when a march of internees accompanied by a band was seen as an offence to those who had lost relatives in the war.

'Lancaster Camp, 7.15am … Appell' (rollcall, used here humorously). Watercolour by Adolph Ernest Jean von du Stratton, 1915. (LCM)

By 1915 the camp on Caton Road was no longer deemed an appropriate location: internees across the nation were being relocated to Knockaloe Aliens Camp on the Isle of Man, and locally the National Projectile Factory was being built beside the camp on Caton Road. In the same year, civilian prisoners were removed from the gaol at Lancaster Castle, which was to provide accommodation for German prisoners of war, detached from the camp at Leigh, who formed working parties in the area.

Three German prisoners who died in April 1919 of influenza-related complications were buried in Lancaster Cemetery, where they were interred with military honours. As the *Lancaster Guardian* reported on 12 April 1919, their coffins were covered with German flags, with a wreath placed on each. The coffins were conveyed in three hearses which were accompanied by six

This carved bone features a rose and leaves and is marked '1914 Remembrance 1915' and 'Made in POW Camp, Vieteck, 1803, Lancaster'. (KOM)

comrades as wreath bearers, and by three guards. The towns-people were reported as showing 'sympathetic interest' and the cortege was met on the way to the cemetery by a firing party from the barracks.

Life on the home front

There is ample evidence that Lancastrians who remained at home found ways of expressing their patriotism and commitment to the war effort in myriad ways. On outbreak of war, young men were paid to guard railway bridges for fear of alien sabotage and the population was alert to the dangers of internal enemies and spy activity as is evidenced by the reporting of suspicious lights on Morecambe sea front and in the fells, or a car 'suspiciously' left without number plates in Lancaster. The Mayoress, Mary Alice Briggs, purportedly set up sewing parties twice a week, where she presided over 150 women, not putting any seamstresses out of work, however. She also gifted beef tea to the Infirmary, joined a Voluntary Aid Detachment (VAD) and sent comforts to the troops. Conversely, Caroline Marshall, the suffragist and peace activist, stood up against 'our sort' as she put it, for Conscientious Objectors (COs), giving a temporary home to the CO William Hayes.

The large numbers of soldiers in town also brought negative consequences. From very early in the war there was an increase in the number of cases brought to the police courts of men and women charged with drunkenness or disorderly conduct. One of the excuses was that the men were reservists, on the way to the depot of their regiments, and had been 'treated' by friends, or were having a jollification before taking up arms. The defendants received no sympathy by the courts, who stated that their actions were quite out of harmony with the spirit of the country which had taken up the struggle. The prevalence of drunkenness led to the suggestion that public houses might very well be closed earlier each night, or open later each morning.

A case before Lancaster's magistrates saw the conviction of Hannah Mary Morland, age 24, wife of a Territorial soldier,

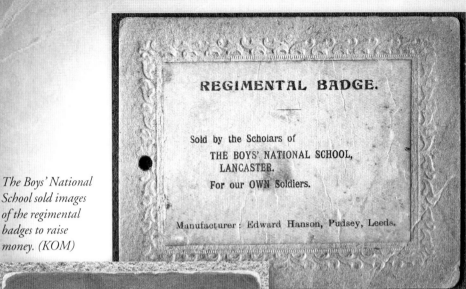

The Boys' National School sold images of the regimental badges to raise money. (KOM)

living at 3 James Street. She was found guilty of keeping a brothel. Chief Constable Harriss prosecuted the case. He told the court that Morland's husband was away with the 5th Battalion of the King's Own, and since he had been away she had been carrying out this business, and more recently she had been assisted by other women. As many as three houses had been under observation by the police and different men had been seen very late at night. A disturbance in James Street resulted when some soldiers of the Royal Welch Fusiliers, posted to guard the Wagon Works, spent the night at the house, and the neighbourhood was up in arms about it. Captain Fairclough, of the Royal Welch, addressed the magistrates and stated that he had great difficulty in keeping the men at the Wagon Works, stating they gave more trouble than the prisoners owing to the number of girls constantly hanging around the place. He described how two girls got inside the works the other day, spent the night in the place and were lifted over the wall by soldiers next morning.

The Mayor, William Briggs, as the chief magistrate, said it was a very demoralising and shocking state of affairs, and any action the military authorities might take would have the support of the Bench, who were determined to try and stop these activities going on in Lancaster. Mrs Morland was sent to the Castle gaol for two months' hard labour. History does not record the reaction of Private Morland in Didcot who must have been quick to learn about his wife's activities as a full report appeared in the *Lancaster Guardian*, copies of which were sure to find their way to Didcot.

The impact of the war on children is elusive in the primary sources, but should not be ignored. At the start of 1915, Panikos Panayi notes that of the 2,000 internees in Caton Road Camp, 200 were boys under seventeen, some of whom had been taken from fishing boats. Wolff also mentions boys being interned in the camp, eighteen of whom being discharged in December 1914, along with five missionaries. As far as local children are concerned, Bulmer's 1912 directory for Lancaster lists nineteen academies and schools as well as the Storey Institute and Museum, an art, technical and science school. Apart from providing recruits from amongst pupils, former pupils and staff, schools also supported the war effort in a variety of ways. The Boys' and Girls' Grammar Schools both had school magazines during the war. While the boys shared news from 'Old Lancastrians' on the battlefront and founded an Officer Training Corps, the Girls' magazine was a rich source on life on the home front, including, for example, the accounts of a Belgian refugee who attended the school, of fundraising activities to support a prisoner of war and the foundation of Westfield War Memorial Village. The girls also mourned with their headmistress, Miss Phillimore, when she lost one of her three serving brothers to wounds received in action.

THE LANCASTER GIRLS' GRAMMAR SCHOOL

The origins of the Girls' Grammar School lie in the Pupil Teacher Centre intended to train Pupil Teachers at the end of the eighteenth century. Its history has been recorded by Pat Harrison, former Head of History at the school. In 1901 the Centre moved to the Storey Institute and a few years later these Centres had been merged into Secondary Schools. The Lancaster Girls' Grammar School (LGGS) adopted that name in January 1908: its location near the train station allowed girls to attend from surrounding areas, from Lunesdale to Garstang. The Storey Institute became too small to house the growing intake of pupils and a new building was erected on Regent Street, the school moving in on 22 September 1914, after the outbreak of war. With various additions, that building remains the heart of the current LGGS.

The impact of the war on the school was reflected in myriad ways: school hours were altered to reflect lighting restrictions; certificates were awarded instead of prizes to support War Savings; the girls raised money for numerous war-related causes, from the Serbian Relief Fund to the Jack Cornwell VC Memorial Fund; their excursions included a trip on Empire Day to see a cinematographic show entitled 'Britain Prepared' and a month's flax-pulling in Shropshire; and they adopted two prisoners of war. The war work of Old Girls included employment in agriculture and munitions, clerical work on the railway and voluntary work. The girls were informed by the Chairman of the Lancashire Education Committee, Henry Hibbert, that 'never has the country needed more trained and educated women'. For some, however, the war ended their education: in 1914, for example, three girls were unable to return to school because of changes in their home circumstances 'due to the war'.

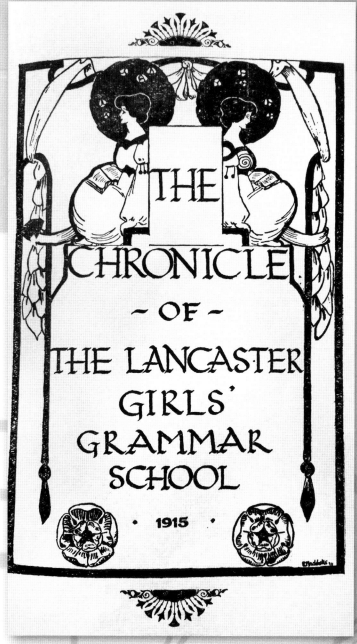

A wartime edition of The Chronicle of the Girls' Grammar School, *first published in 1914. (CPB with kind permission from LGGS)*

Industry and employment

At the outbreak of war, the two civilian employers who dominated the Lancaster landscape were James Williamson & Son
and Storey Brothers. Bulmer's trade directory of 1912 described
the products of the former as including linoleum, floor cloth,
table baize, leathercloth and varnish manufacturers, with sites
at St George's Works (now derelict) and Lune Mills (now rede-
veloped as housing), St George's Quay, and cotton spinners and
manufacturers located at Greenfield Mills (the last mill to be
built in Lancaster in 1864) and Bath Mills, Moor Lane (acquired
by Williamson's in 1864). As Lancaster's Civic Society explains,
table baize was a woven covering for tables (and other surfaces);
leathercloth was calico-coated with linseed oil and embossed
to make a covering similar to leather, and oilcloth was an early
waterproofed cotton textile. Storey Brothers similarly produced
leathercloth and table baize manufacturing, and was also listed
as cotton spinner and manufacturer, with sites at White Cross
(where Lancaster's oldest mill opened in 1802), just one of a
line of mills that stretched along the canal from Queen Street
Mill (now B&Q) in the south, to Albion Mill, Bulk Road, in the
north. These mills were used in the manufacture of, for example,
grey cotton that was subsequently used as a backing material for
oilcloth. It was at Queen's Mill, where Anaglypta wall coverings
were first manufactured.

James Helme & Co. (the father of Norval Watson Helme, the
Liberal MP for Lancaster during the war) ran Halton Mills which
manufactured oilcloth, baize and leathercloth. Lord Ashton and
Herbert Lushington Storey were other principal landowners in
the area. There were also multiple stained glass window manufacturers: Abbott Jas. Hartley at 27 West Road, for example, Jas.
Holmes. & Co. on Fenton Street, and perhaps most famously
Shrigley & Hunt on 23 Castle Hill, which was to gain further
commissions creating stained glass window memorials for the
fallen. A great tension in the war was the competing needs of the
military and the civilian professions: the case of Williamson's as
outlined by Philip Gooderson provides a clear local example of

Storey Brothers of Lancaster, White Cross. (LCM)

the challenges employers faced. By January 1915, 900 men from Williamson's had volunteered – over one fifth of the workforce. Replacing all of these with women could not be assured especially after the opening of the higher paying Caton Road and White Lund munitions works, although oral testimony suggests some parents refused to let their daughters work at these.

After the call for volunteers that followed the heavy casualties of the First Battle of Ypres the preceding autumn, in the spring of 1915, Lord Ashton wrote to the War Office stating that he would not be able to keep his works open if more men joined up (see Chapter 2). Norval Helme and Storey expressed their solidarity, but the War Office suggested that enlistment 'is purely a matter for the men to decide for themselves'. When that ceased to be the case following the introduction of conscription in the Military Service Act of January 1916, the local tribunals were not averse to offering temporary exemptions to employees of the oilcloth firms. This perhaps reflected an awareness of the importance of keeping the works open for the sake of the town, rather than their contributions to the war effort: Williamson's produced blackout curtains. It was the floor coverings, however, which ensured

The Royal Visit to Lancaster's munitions factories, May 1917. (KOM)

the industry was upgraded from 'non-essential' to 'restricted', as these were favoured by the medical profession and the Red Cross for hygiene reasons. Nonetheless, by 1917, production was down to around a quarter of 1914 levels: Lord Ashton had lost 41 per cent of his male workforce to the military and 24 per cent to munitions work, and of his pre-war force of women cotton workers, 42 per cent had left, often to munitions which offered better pay and the lure of the Royal Visit in 1917.

Other local industries shifted production more substantially. By the summer of 1915, a scheme of co-operative aircraft construction had been rolled out from Scotland to England, using small sub-contractors for the manufacture of aeroplane parts: Waring and Gillow was renowned for its cabinet furniture, but in the First World War, the Lancaster factory switched to making products for the war effort. There are photographic records showing women working on biplane wings in the factory in Lancaster, located on North Road, and the company records also reveal that it manufactured ammunition chests for the Navy and propellers for De Havilland DH9 aircraft.

In Lancashire, women were already an integral part of the labour force as they were heavily employed in the textile industry. There is, however, evidence that there was a new influx of women into the major employers of Lancaster, Storey's and Williamson's, as the men departed for war. Lancaster exemplified Gail Braybon's theory that the greatest impact of the First World War on women's work was not to introduce it, but to make it visible. For example, the electric buses taking workers to the munitions works on Caton Road left from the centre of town, in front of the Old Town Hall in Market Square. There were no bus conductresses in Lancaster until the end of the war: it was not until mid-1918 that agreement could be reached over appropriate clothing for them.

Battery-powered electric buses are seen here in Market Square in c. 1917, picking up female workers to take them to the Caton Road Works. (LCM)

In 1914 there were sixteen firms nationally with munitions contracts with the War Office; by the end of the war there were over 218 new or adapted factories producing every kind of

Staff at the White Lund Filling Factory. (LCM)

munitions. Two of those were in Lancaster – Vickers Ltd managed the National Projectile Factory (NPF) on Caton Road and the National Filling Factory (NFF) on the White Lund, Morecambe. Construction had begun on the former in September 1915, and the site opened in November 1916. Manufacturing and related work here included grenade mortars, 9.2in, 6in, 8in and 60-pounder shells, plus repair and trench warfare work. By the end of the war, the NPF employed 8,656 employees, 53 per cent of whom were men. This statistic is an important reminder that the majority of the male population remained on the home front – and that civilians could take pride in their contribution to the battlefront.

Poems from 'N.P.F. Lancaster', sold to raise money for St Dunstan's Hostel for the Blind, express this pride in humorous tones, for example, in an ode to the 9.2in shell:

The work is done, now we must part
And for our native town shall start
To leave behind, what we know well,
The making of the 9.2 shell.

A 'Ripping' time when on 'Rough Turn',
And what a wage 'Nose Bore' could earn.
Then 'Inside Bore' and 'Finish Turn',
That good old 9.2 shell.

Construction of the NFF began on 23 November 1915, and the site opened in July 1916, encompassing sixteen bonded stores, a paint shop, a shell store, magazines, a power station, and six 'danger' huts. 6in howitzers, 8in High Explosives (HE) and 60-pounder HE were filled here with Amatol, a mixture of TNT and ammonium nitrate, or gas. Women outnumbered male employees at this establishment: in September 1917, they constituted 64.4 per cent of the 4,621 employees.

The workers were accommodated in local lodgings rather than attracting new building projects to house them, as was the case in some other new factories such as the one at Gretna. The work was dangerous, but comparatively well-paid. Deaths were caused by poisoning (by gas or TNT), and industrial accidents: there were three fatalities caused by accidents involving cranes, for example.

The site remained dangerous. On 5 April 1918 a team of 13 men were salvaging shells from the units wrecked in 1917. Two were killed in an explosion. Then on 14 January 1920, there was another explosion as staff defused and emptied shells. Nine were killed.

The NFF covered a 400-acre site. The number of separate small wooden huts was intended to contain the risk of explosions. (LCM)

Both munitions factories offered new opportunities for female employment. This image shows Miss Susannah Thompson in uniform, NPF. (LCM)

The Lancaster Munitions Tribunal began meeting from October 1916 to rule on issues concerning either of the munitions factories. Of particular concern were infractions of the prohibition to smuggle matches or cigarettes on to the premises, given the risk of explosive accidents; petty crime including theft was also ruled on here. In 1916, the YMCA on China Street began a club for munitions workers; perhaps in response to national fears about the drinking and courting behaviours of the young female workers. This was not entirely without foundation: in Lancaster three female munitions workers were sentenced for running a brothel on the side. But there is also evidence of sexual innocence: the Imperial War Museum holds a manuscript by Olive Taylor who left Yorkshire to fill shells on the White Lund. She lived in lodgings in Morecambe at 25s a week (out of wages of 27s) and 'slept five in a room and never got enough to eat.' She was so horrified to find out how babies were made that her workmates began to call her 'Old Molly never had it'. The workers also developed their own forms of entertainment: the NPF had both a Vaudeville Society and a Projectile Club which offered such entertainments as vaudeville reviews (such as 'Hullo Projectile' in May 1917), or a fancy dress dance to mark the second anniversary of the factory opening.

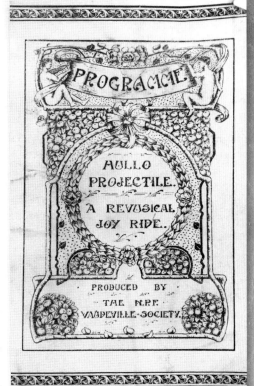

The programme cover for the NPF revue 'Hullo Projectile'. (CPB)

The White Lund disaster

At 10.15 p.m. on 1 October 1917, a fire was spotted in Unit 6c at the National Filling Factory. The upper floor held large amounts of TNT; the lower floor, 12-inch partially filled shells which exploded about twenty minutes after the fire began. As the majority of the workers were still in the canteen on their break, most managed to escape unharmed or with minor injuries, despite the panicked rush to the gates (which initially could not be opened because of the crush) and the danger of falling into the flooded marshes around the site. The explosions, the largest of which occurred at 3.00 a.m., could be heard and seen across the region: ornaments fell from mantelpieces, windows smashed, and ceilings collapsed. Shrapnel from the explosion was found as far away as Scotforth and Quernmore. Many of the local populace took to the hills and surrounding areas, although many such as Morecambe promenade proved to be unsafe with shells exploding overhead and shrapnel raining down. One man (anonymised as Mr K1L), interviewed by Elizabeth Roberts in the 1970s, recalled how as a child he and his siblings had walked all the way to Caton to get away from the explosions, being passed by an ice cream man:

> He had five or six kids and he had them sitting on top of a bassinet and he said, 'Me no stop me go on.' And he landed at Hornby.
>
> *Did a lot of people go away?*
>
> Yes, you'd go as far away from it as you could, because you didn't know what was happening. We thought it was a Zeppelin dropping bombs. They could hear it at Bentham. An aunt of mine heard it at Bentham. We slept on the bare floor with just a blanket round us in Caton Institute.

Contemporary public reports were kept deliberately curt. Records suggest that ten men were killed that night, mainly fighting the fires. Four Edward Medals were won – introduced to award bravery in 'Mines' and 'Industry' – with each type having a Silver and Bronze version. Of the 188 Industry medals awarded, only twenty-five Silver awards were made between 1907 and 1949 – four of which were for the explosion at the White Lund. Two recipients were Thomas Kew and Abraham Graham who shunted twenty-nine, forty-nine or fifty-five ammunition trucks (sources vary) holding 250,000 live shells out of the danger zone. The other two were Thomas Tattershall, the works' fireman, and Police Sergeant Thomas Coppard who shepherded 300 workers to safety. The telephonist Mary Agnes Wilkinson was awarded the Medal of the Order of the British Empire (MOBE) for her devotion to duty. She cycled through the chaos to the exchange in Cable Street. She was blown off her bicycle twice on the way, and stayed at her post for twenty-four hours. Lily Cope, a nurse on duty in the ambulance room at the filling factory, was also awarded a MOBE in November 1918. She stayed with an injured man for six-and-a-half hours in the chaos of the factory grounds, and then succeeded in having him removed to the Royal

Three Edward Medal holders leaving Buckingham Palace after receiving their medals on 7 May 1918. (L-R: Graham, Coppard, Kew). (LCM)

Lancaster Infirmary. A third medal was won by the factory nurse Maisie Shepherd who perfomed 'her duties quietly and without regard to personal safety'. The local families supplementing their income lost their lodgers overnight: the factory was not to reopen fully during the war.

Rumours abounded about the cause of the explosion: initially locals assumed a Zeppelin attack, not such a fanciful idea given that on 25 September 1916, Rawtenstall, Holcombe and Bolton had all been bombed from the air. Anne Spencer (née Harrington), who witnessed the explosions at the age of 10, described how her Aunt and Uncle in Manchester 'were frantic because they could see the fire and hear the explosions (almost 80 miles away) and were told that the whole of Morecambe and Lancaster were in ruins and they were walking on the dead'. Another theory suggested the fire had been the result of the actions of a German agent working in the TNT store, although the police scoffed at the idea he could have smuggled in matches. Graham Pedder maintained for decades afterwards that the agent had smuggled them in under his eyepatch. At the inquest of Willing Topping, the jury returned the following verdict: 'That deceased's death was due to injuries accidentally received while carrying out his duties during a fire in a national filling factory, there being no evidence to how the fire originated.' It seems unlikely we will ever have any certainty as to the cause.

Conclusions

Life on the home front was a curious mixture of the familiar and the novel; the continuities of labour and pleasure activities and their disruption by the demands of war. Responses to the war were also contradictory: on the one hand, there was a hunger for news from the front, on the other hand, escapist film and literature untouched by martial themes remained highly popular – Mary Pickford was not just 'America's Sweetheart', as local reviews of her films testify. The impact of the war ranged from the irritating and inconvenient – such as lighting restrictions – and at the other extreme, the devastation of bereavement. This was true across Britain. In Lancaster, the profile of employment and the presence of the King's Own created some distinct consequences. As the following chapters show, the war was substantially to change the profile of the city.

4

FROM THE FRONT: THE KING'S OWN EXPERIENCE

To give a flavour of the experience of Lancastrian soldiers, this chapter describes three of the main events in which members of the King's Own were involved. After all, 40 per cent of Lancastrians who died in the war died with the King's Own. The first of these events is the 1914 Retreat from Mons. The British Expeditionary Force, newly arrived in France, found itself in the way of the major German advance that swept through Belgium and then south towards Paris. This led to desperate fighting in which the King's Own's 1st Battalion paid a heavy price. This successful defence led to the failure of the German Schlieffen Plan but, in turn, paved the way for the trench warfare that would last until 1918. The second, in 1915, saw the 1st/5th and 2nd Battalions of the King's Own heavily involved in the Second Battle of Ypres in which the Germans used poison gas for the first time on the Western Front. Ultimately, the German attack was a failure but, as described in Chapter 5, this fighting led to Lancaster's worst period of the war. The Second Battle of Ypres has largely been forgotten by the history books. The third battle discussed here is that of the Somme in 1916, which, by contrast, has become the archetypal British First World War battle. Five battalions of the regiment were involved.

The German plan of attack was named after their chief-of-staff Alfred von Schlieffen. It reflected the belief that Germany would have to contend with a war on two fronts: with France in the west and Russia in the east. The intention was to beat France rapidly, then turn to meet the Russian army, which would take longer to mobilise. In 1914, the plan swiftly went awry when Russia began to mobilise before France, and Britain declared war on Germany for the invasion of Belgium.

The Battle of Le Cateau

The 1st Battalion, King's Own, travelled across the English Channel on board the *SS Saturnia* on 22 August 1914. Their Commanding Officer, Lieutenant Colonel Alfred McNair Dykes was annoyed to be placed in command of all the troops on board the ship, as he explained in what would turn out to be the last letter he would write to his wife. Whilst he was writing the letter, some of his soldiers on board found an empty beer bottle of the Crown Brewery at Fulham and wrote a quick note, placed it in the bottle and threw it over board. The message was not read until it was caught in the nets of the Grimsby trawler *Egret* on 6 March 1922:

> From the boys of the King's Own (R.L.R.), Dover, SS Saturnia. 22nd August 1914
> To The Editor, The Daily Mirror
> Well on the way to the front. Just seen the last of England. Mean to fight like Britons. Hope to see Leicester Square again shortly.

The battalion arrived in France on 23 August 1914 and, moving by train and route march, arrived at the village of Haucourt on the morning of 26 August. Their orders were to hold the

The SS Saturnia *on which the 1st Battalion, King's Own, crossed the English Channel on 22 August 1914.* (KOM)

The shell-encrusted beer bottle thrown into the sea by soldiers on board the SS Saturnia *and picked up by the Grimsby trawler* Egret *on 6 March 1922, containing a hand-written note to the Editor of the* Daily Mirror. *(KOM)*

German advance, as the British Expeditionary Force was pushed back from the Belgian city of Mons. The men were exhausted and hungry, so as breakfast was prepared, the battalion formed up on a forward-facing slope. The sergeant majors ensured that the lines were smart, neat and tidy. The decision was also taken that the men should have their 'arms piled', which means that the rifles were placed with their butts on the ground with their muzzles leaning on each other.

Second Lieutenant Gaston Roland Rigden Beaumont, who had been commissioned into the 3rd (Special Reserve) Battalion of the King's Own in 1913 and attached to the 1st Battalion on mobilisation, provides an account of the events that followed. In the fighting, the battalion was nearly destroyed as a fighting unit, Lieutenant Colonel Dykes and many others were killed, and many more, including Lieutenant Charles Irving (see Chapter 1), wounded or taken prisoner:

> We arrived at dawn by the Ligny Road to a spot where subsequently we suffered so heavily. The Battalion was ordered to form close Column facing the enemy's direction of defences. Companies were dressed by the right, piled arms, and placed equipment at their feet. There was a big stir because some of the arms were out of alignment and the equipment did not in all cases show

a true line. A full 7 to 10 minutes was spent in adjusting these errors. The Brigade Commander rode up to the Commanding Officer (Lieutenant Colonel Dykes) and shortly afterwards we were told to remain where we were as breakfast would shortly be up. Everyone was very tired and hungry having had nothing to eat since dinner the day before. A remark was passed as regards our safety. My Company Commander replied that French Cavalry were out in front and the enemy could not possibly worry us for at least three hours.

The picture of this period was as follows:

Three Companies of the Battalion in close Column, the fourth company just about to move up to the left with a view to continuing a line with the 20th who had just commenced to dig in. Just about this time some Cavalry (about a troop) rode within 500 yards of us, looked at us and trotted off again. I saw their uniform quite distinctly and mentioned that they were not Frenchmen. I was told not to talk nonsense and reminded that I was very young. It was early in the morning and nobody felt talkative, least of all my Company Commander. The Cavalry appeared again in the distance and brought up wheeled vehicles; this was all done very peaceably and exposed to full view. We could now hear the road transport on the cobbled road and a shout went up 'Here's the Cooker'. New life came to the men and mess tins were hurriedly sought. Then came the fire. The field we were in was a cornfield. The corn had been cut. Bullets were mostly about 4 feet high just hitting the top of the corn stalks. Temporary panic ensued. Some tried to reach the valley behind, others chewed the cud; of those who got up most were hit. The machine gun fire only lasted about two minutes and caused about 400 casualties. The 4th Company moving off to the left was caught in columns of fours. Shell fire now started and did considerable damage to the transport,

Corporal Ellis Williams (left), 1st Battalion, King's Own, at Waterloo Station, London following his evacuation from France. (KOM)

the cooker being the first vehicle to go. A little Sealyham terrier that we had collected at Horsham St. Faith's before embarking, and that the troops had jacketed with the Union Jack was killed whilst standing next to the Driver of a General Service Wagon. I mention this as I saw the same Driver the day after still carrying the dog, he was very upset when he was ordered to bury it.

The Commanding Officer was killed by the first burst and the Second in Command rallied the Battalion; several of us taking up position to the right of the point where we had suffered so heavily.

An attack was organised at once, we re-took our arms and got in most of the wounded. The others were left and taken prisoner later at Haucourt Church that night.

Never again on active service was any battalion of the King's Own given the order to 'pile arms'.

The fighting from this period at the Battle of Le Cateau inspired one of Lancaster's sons, the poet Laurence Binyon, born on High Street, Lancaster, in 1869, to write his poem *For the Fallen*. This was published in *The Times* newspaper on 21 September 1914, long before the full horrors of the conflict emerged. The verse ending 'We will remember them' forms a central part in Remembrance Day activities today.

Corporal Ellis Williams, a long-time member of the battalion, was wounded at Le Cateau and evacuated home. Writing from the London Hospital on 1 December, he described the action in a letter home to his mother:

I have landed here after a short tour round France. I am wounded in the right forearm (shell) but nothing serious. They think I have got a touch of dysentery but I doubt it myself. I can't write about our engagement for it would fill a book. Tell Dad (former Colour Sergeant Ellis Williams) it was a great blunder. Our brigade formed in mass on a hill and entrenched to oppose the German right flank. We had no sooner formed mass when the Germans opened fire with about 15 Maxims and 4 Brigades of artillery at a distance of about 350 to 500 yards. All we could do was to lie down flat on our faces, but the fire got too hot and we had to return to a small village. They then directed their fire on the village and completely destroyed it. Our Colonel and many officers were killed and, they say, nearly half the Battalion. I did not see Jack [his brother] so God only knows if he is safe. We must pray that he is so ... I have no arms or equipment. I took them to the Field Hospital but they shelled it so we had to leave. Some poor chaps were buried in it. Poor Jack Sharp was one I believe. I should like some cigarettes for I'm broke absolutely. I have asked Fred to get me a razor and some more things and I will pay him later.
No more at present. Mother.
Best Love to all.
Your affectionate son.
Ellis.

Corporal Williams's brother, Sergeant John (Jack) Williams was, in fact, taken prisoner

Five Williams brothers, from Hanmer Place, Bowerham, served in the War. While Ellis and Jack survived, Herbert died of wounds in France, 23 March 1915; Reginald was killed on the Somme, 12 October 1916; and Lloyd drowned when his boat sank on the River Nile in May 1917.

and was able to send a postcard home to his parents who lived at Bowerham. The card, dated 16 October 1914, stated:

> I am in a large hospital in Berlin (Templehof Garrison), and arrived here on Sunday from Doberitz. I was wounded on 26th August in the right thigh at Harcourt, in France. Was, of course, taken prisoner, as I could not move, and sent back to Ligny, in Belgium, under a German guard. I remained there three weeks and then moved to Cambrai, and so by train through Germany to Dobertiz, some 12 miles from Berlin. Here my wound took a turn for the worse, and I was operated upon for abscess, and, unfortunately, they struck an artery. I remained in hospital at Dobertiz, but, with its only being an improvised hospital they could do me no good. Anyhow, I was taken to Berlin last Sunday (11th October) and was again operated upon on the following Tuesday, and am now doing very well. When you write, write on an open postcard. I don't know how long I shall be here. I am dying to hear from someone.

Despite the carnage suffered by the 1st Battalion, King's Own, at Le Cateau, 26 August 1914, only two Lancastrians were killed: John Arkwright (47 Clarence Street) and Thomas Henderson (84 Clarendon Road). Edward Armer (15 Ridge Street) of the King's Own Yorkshire Light Infantry was also killed that day. They were the first three Lancastrians killed in action during the War.

Jack Williams remained a prisoner of war until after the Armistice in November 1918 when he was repatriated.

After Le Cateau, the 1st Battalion retreated into France with the rest of the Expeditionary Force. The time was very trying with the constant threat of German attack. There was no rest and little to eat except the emergency rations. When the battalion crossed the River Somme all officers' kits were burnt to allow for the transport to be used by the wounded and the foot-sore men, showing just how much pressure the men were under. By 29 August 1914 the strength of the battalion had fallen to fourteen officers and 400 other ranks, under half the numbers which had arrived in France less than a week earlier.

The Second Battle of Ypres

Lancaster's Territorial Force battalion, now designed the 1st/5th Battalion, King's Own Royal Lancaster Regiment, departed England on St Valentine's Day 1915, on board the *Manchester Importer*, another merchant vessel hired by the War Office for use in the conflict. Private Robert Higginson, a 'Lancaster Pal' and formerly a clerk with the London and North Western Railway at Lancaster Castle station, described the journey across the channel as having conditions like a cattle boat, with rotten sleeping accommodation and noting that he was rather seasick. The boat arrived at Le Havre at 7.00 a.m., however, it was not until after noon that it finally berthed and the soldiers were able to disembark in France.

They began their journey to the Front, starting with a four-mile route march to the station and a train with forty to forty-five men to each cattle truck. It was a horrible journey which ended up with a 7-mile march to tented accommodation. By 20 February the men were digging practice trenches and by Sunday 14 March they were getting ready to move into the front line trenches. 'Lancaster Pal' Private Frank Cantrill described the scene on 30 March:

> When you look over the parapet you can see ruined houses all the way around and great big big holes where the shells have dropped. One house is only fifty yards away, and two of us went off to look round for some coal for our fire and it was a sight to see, dead horses, cows, and pigs all over the place. There were about a dozen men buried in the garden at the back of the house.

On 9 April, the battalion was moved to the Ypres salient and took up positions in Polygon Wood, east of the town. They received their first shock of a German attack on 13 and 14 April. Major Bates, the battalion's second in command, wrote home to a friend:

13th April – the trench mortars caught a number of our chaps. The next night a working party were in the woods and high explosive shells were pushed into them. In twenty seconds four were killed and twenty were wounded. Blackhurst and Fred Eltoft hit by a trench mortar and didn't live long.

The Colonel takes the service and I accompany him, apart from the pioneers who make the graves, and the stretcher bearers, we are alone. It was a sad affair, noisy through the booming of heavy guns and rifle cracking all around.

We soon forget it all, but however horrible is the war we realise we are fighting for posterity, and we pray it will soon be over.

Lance Corporal John Hirst Harper, 1st/5th Battalion, King's Own, killed in action 13 April 1915. One of those on the sketch map on page 84 and one of a number of brothers who feature on Lancaster's War Memorial. (KOM)

While they were there they were heavily shelled. One of the 'Pals' wrote home:

We just got into the centre of the wood when the Germans started shelling it. Well, we had to take any cover we could get, and I tumbled over a dead horse, it's ribs went in but I laid where I was, till another shell brought the top of a tree down, and it caught me fair on the 'thinking box' and I made my way out of the wood after the nerve testing experience with a champion head.

War is simply hell let loose. There has been over 50 killed and wounded in less than 24 hours. You feel it when your mates go down.

Another Lancaster soldier wrote home:

> We have moved to a place called by the regulars the 'Gates of Hell'. No picture nor pen can describe it ... as Lancaster will soon know our casualties in the two days are eight killed and about forty wounded.

When the men were relieved from Polygon Wood and pulled back to billets in Ypres Lunatic Asylum on 17 April, Lord Richard Cavendish wrote in his diary:

> Our total casualties for the four days were 14 killed or died of wounds and 44 wounded. Three men's nerves went and George (Medical Officer) fears that two may be permanently mad. The men are very cheerful ...

Private Carr of the 1st/5th Battalion, King's Own, watches as shells explode overhead near the Menin Road, Ypres. (KOM)

Casualties were buried in graves marked with hastily created wooden crosses. Until soldiers were issued with two fibre identity

discs from 1916, no identity disk remained with the body once interred, as the metal identity disk in use at the time of this battle was removed from the body once the grave marker named the soldier. However, the terrain and many of these graves were subsequently destroyed by the fighting that continued in this area for much of the rest of the war, even if attempts had been made to record burials. This explains why so many of the men killed have no known grave and so many of First World War headstones simply read 'A soldier of the Great War known unto God.'

If the news of those killed and wounded in the shelling at Polygon Wood was a shock to Lancaster, worse was to come within only a few days. On 21 April, the 1st/5th Battalion was by now dug in north of St Jean, near Ypres, where they caught some of the German shelling. Steams of panic-stricken civilians and green-faced gasping French soldiers and Zouvaves (French colonial troops) came straggling back, obviously panic-stricken, not wounded, but suffering terribly and quite incoherent. These were some of the very few survivors of the first German gas attack, when the line held by the French Territorials and Zouaves had been overwhelmed and routed. On 23 April, St George's Day which was also the Regiment's Day, the 1st/5th acted as a supporting battalion to an attack, but they had only the vaguest outlines as to the objectives and the direction. Colonel Lord Richard Cavendish described what happened:

We got under rifle fire, there was not a particle of cover, the leading regiment lost direction, and we got enfilade fire on us. I was pleased with the way our fellows went ahead, continually meeting a stream of wounded going to the rear and the ground littered with dead. There was one field with heaps of manure in rows. A lot of fellows thought that they could take shelter behind them. They are, of course not bullet-proof, and there was hardly a heap without a dead or wounded man beside it. The opium tablets came in very handy. I gave a lot to the poor fellows.

Sketch map showing the location of graves of soldiers of the 1st/5th Battalion, King's Own, killed at Polygon Wood in April 1915. (KOM)

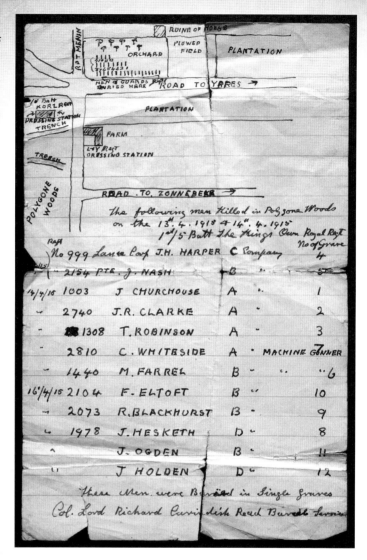

The Colonel then described the scene after the battle:

> It was a terrible experience going over the battlefield last night – dead men, rifles, packs, equipment, lying at all directions. We have not been able to bury many of them as our spades have been left far away from our trenches. I am glad to say that a good many of our missing have turned up. The men are wonderfully good at the way they go on.

The following day, Private James Radcliffe Mawson died of wounds. He was the son of Thomas Mawson, a landscape architect. As Chapter 8 describes, his son's death motivated Thomas Mawson to suggest the scheme which resulted in the construction of Westfield War Memorial Village.

The battle continued into early May with the 1st/5th Battalion continuing to take casualties. On 3 May the 1st/5th was moved to a hamlet called Frezenburg about 5 miles east of Ypres where it spent several days being heavily shelled. The battalion was pulled back to reserve trenches on 6 May when it were relieved by the 2nd Battalion, King's Own, which was serving in the same brigade. On 8 May the Germans attacked the Frezenburg trenches in what turned out to be their last major offensive of Second Ypres.

> About 12 Major Clough and about 40 men of the 2nd Battalion came in and told us that the Germans had attacked that morning in overwhelming strength and had taken the trenches, and that they were the only survivors of the Battalion. (R. Cavendish, qu. in *The King's Own*)

The 1st/5th and some of the survivors of the 2nd Battalion were then involved in another counterattack which again failed with heavy losses. The casualties included Lieutenant Stanley Bates, Major Bates' son (see also Chapter 7), who was killed, and Colonel Lord Richard Cavendish, who was wounded. Major Bates, the battalion's second-in-command, had been invalided home a few days previously. Neither Colonel Lord Cavendish nor Major Bates returned to the battalion.

The 1st/5th's casualties from 9 April to 11 May were 7 officers and 113 men killed and 14 officers and 416 men wounded. The battalion's war diary notes that on the night of 11 May 'the survivors of the

Private James Radcliffe (Cliffe) Mawson of the 1st/5th Battalion, King's Own, died of wounds in the Second Battle of Ypres on St George's Day, 1915. (KOM)

85

Battalion, over 1,000 strong coming out, now slept in a hut and a very small barn.'

The Battle of the Somme

The King's Own was heavily involved in the 141 day long Battle of the Somme in 1916. On the first day of the battle, 1 July 1916, the 1st Battalion went into action at Serre-Beaumont Hamel. Of the 507 other ranks who went into action on that day, 387 became casualties. They also lost many of their officers, including Major Bromilow who had been in command of the battalion for less than one month. The service battalions, the 7th and 8th Battalions, also both saw bitter fighting, and the two Territorial Battalions, the 1st/4th and Lancaster's own 1st/5th, were frequently in the line and taking part in some of the more mundane duties of trench warfare, providing working parties.

The nature of the regiment and its battalions had changed as the war proceeded, with the Lancastrian flavour being diluted as drafts of men joined to replace the fallen and the wounded. There were, however, Lancaster men still involved in the first days of the battle. Sergeant James Parkinson, of Primrose Hill, Lancaster, was one of the men who left their trenches at 7.30 a.m. and advanced slowly across No Man's Land, as if it was a parade ground drill, and was wounded by shrapnel in the upper part of his thigh when leading a party in bombing attack on the German trenches.

Corporal Jack Davies, a 27-year-old soldier, who lived at Hest Bank with his wife, was wounded in the advance, receiving a compound fracture of the left arm and a severe burn on the right arm. He was quickly evacuated, one of the many thousands of casualties who were, first to Eastleigh Clearing Hospital, near Southampton, and by 8 July was in Trafford Hall Hospital, Manchester.

The 1st/5th Battalion saw relatively little action in July, and their first involvement in the Battle of the Somme was night-time work digging communication trenches. This was an activity certainly not free from risk as the enemy would attempt to disrupt any work that was taking place, and do its best during the day to spot where the work was happening. On 1 August ten officers, twenty-eight non-commissioned officers and 350 other ranks were employed in the trench digging. Two other ranks were killed and seven wounded due to shelling. The work continued for the next couple of days. The loss of one soldier is recorded on 3 August but the German artillery bombardment of 4 August was heavy and claimed one officer wounded, twelve other ranks killed and a further forty wounded, with two men recorded as missing – lost somewhere in the confusion and dark. A similar action followed on the night of 14/15 August when the 1st/5th was ordered to send out 230 men to dig trenches which, at their closest point, came within thirty yards of German trenches. These trenches were to be used as a starting point for a subsequent assault by other units. The night was brightly moonlit and they came under heavy rifle fire. One officer and sixteen other ranks were killed and thirty-four other ranks wounded.

An un-named 'Lancaster Pal' wrote home in a letter dated 15 August:

> It has been hard, dangerous work, all done under heavy shell and rifle fire. Unfortunately our losses were rather large last night, owing to our being so exposed and not having any cover until we had dug ourselves in. I am still fit, safe and sound. We are now about to start our long extended rest. We shall now have an opportunity to settle our nerves and enjoy our rest and parcels.

Private Walter Robinson, whose parents lived at 7 Abbey Terrace, Scotforth, wrote home: 'We pioneers have the job of burying the dead, and today we have erected some bonny crosses over three graves.' It is possible that one of these graves was that of Sergeant Herbert Dobson, who had won the military medal for leading a night-time patrol in December 1915, and was Lancaster's first King's Scout. He was killed on 9 August 1916 at Trones Wood, and was buried by his battalion. The grave was marked with a

ANTHONY HOYLE

Anthony Hoyle was born in Overton, Lancashire, in 1875 of Elizabeth (née Maloy) and Anthony Hoyle. A veteran of the South African War of 1899–1902, he had served with an Active Service Company of the King's Own Volunteer Battalion. By civilian occupation a plasterer's labourer for T. & J. Till, in the First World War he enlisted in Lancaster and served in the 1st Battalion. He was wounded on 6 July 1916. Although heavily cut up on 1 July, the battalion had to remain in the front line for a full ten days to hold off German coun-terattacks. Hoyle was admitted to the Base Hospital, but died of his wounds on 12 July in the 2nd Stationery Hospital. He is buried in St Sever Cemetery, Rouen, in keeping with the British policy not to repatriate bodies. In the war, camps and hospitals were stationed on the southern outskirts of Rouen. The hospitals included eight general, five stationary, one British Red Cross, one labour hospital, and No. 2 Convalescent Depot. Although some of the dead from these hospitals were buried in other cemeteries, the majority were taken to the city cemetery of St Sever which had to be extended in September 1916. The cemetery contains 3082 burials of individuals from the Commonwealth, one French burial and one non-service burial from the war. Sergeant Hoyle left a widow who resided at 16 Primrose Street, Lancaster, and six children, the eldest of whom was serving with the Lancashire Fusiliers at Colchester.

Soldiers of the 1st/4th Battalion, King's Own, on the Somme, 1916, Lewis Gun Teams. (KOM)

The hand-painted grave marker of Sergeant Herbert Dobson MM, one of more than 200 hand-painted by Corporal Robert Bell, of the 1st/5th Battalion, King's Own. (KOM)

wooden cross carefully made by the battalion pioneers and hand-painted by Corporal Robert Bell, a painter and decorator before the war, who through the war, carefully painted the details of the deceased soldier on the wooden cross.

The Battle of the Somme continued until 18 November when the whole battle got bogged down in the mud, which eventually froze and made the land harder than ever to move over. The King's Own suffered at least 953 officers and men killed, with an unrecorded number wounded, some of whom would die of their wounds in the coming months and years.

Conclusions

These are only three of the many military actions in which the King's Own were involved during the war. At the start of the war the King's Own consisted of five battalions. Of these, the 3rd (Special Reserve) Battalion remained in the UK throughout the war. The 1st and 1st/5th battalions were moved to France in August 1914 and February 1915 respectively as previously described. The 1st/4th followed them on 3 May 1915. All three were to remain on the Western Front for the rest of the war. The 2nd Battalion, by contrast, which had been rushed back from India at the outbreak of war and fought alongside the 1st/5th at the Second Battle of Ypres, was removed from the Western Front in November 1915 and spent the rest of the war fighting in the Macedonian campaign. Of the battalions formed during the war, the 7th and 8th were both sent to France in 1915 and remained on the Western Front until 1918. The 6th, however, saw action at Gallipoli from July to December 1915 before being moved to Mesopotamia, arriving at Basra on 27 February 1916. They remained in Mesopotamia for the rest of the war. The 9th Battalion spent a brief period in France in the autumn of 1915 before it was moved to Macedonia to fight in the same campaign as the 2nd Battalion.

There was, therefore, fighting in far more places than just the Western Front and the King's Own was involved in much of it. As we will see in the next chapter, Lancastrians fought in many of these battles and campaigns, some of which we remember but many of which have now been all but forgotten.

5

FROM THE FRONT: LANCASTER'S CASUALTIES

The previous chapter discussed some of the major military events of the First World War that involved the King's Own Royal Lancaster Regiment. While the King's Own was based in Lancaster, and the 1st/5th Battalion in particular recruited heavily from the town, many of the men who served and died with the King's Own were not Lancastrians and, similarly, many Lancastrians who served and died did so with units other than the King's Own. Even identifying how many Lancastrians died in the war is difficult. The city's main war memorial, next to the Town Hall (below) lists 1,010 names. The *Reveille* website offers details on 1,055 individuals, as it includes everyone on the war memorial plus some additional people who, for example, had obituaries in the local papers but whose names do not appear on the memorial. This gives us two possible numbers of Lancastrians who died, but neither is definitive.

The Memorial in Lancaster Town Hall Memorial Garden, unveiled in 1924. (ING)

The difficulties are twofold: who is, and is not, a Lancastrian; and how do we define 'killed in the war'? The first of these problems is illustrated by the fact that *Reveille* lists twenty-three Canadians, three Australians, a New Zealander and a South African among its records. Albert Lamb, killed in France with the British Columbia Regiment in June 1918, provides an example of a Canadian Lancastrian. He was born in Burnley but moved to 18 Prospect Street, Lancaster as a child when he also attended Bowerham School. Around the age of 15 he moved to Canada with his parents. After he was killed, aged 21, it is likely that his uncle, Mr S. Foster who lived at 74 Edward Street, was responsible both for his obituary appearing in the *Lancaster Guardian* and his name subsequently appearing on the war memorial. Thus someone who was born in Burnley and died as a Canadian is remember as one of the 'Men of Lancaster who gave their lives in the Great War' to quote the war memorial. It is interesting to speculate how many other men with similar life histories may not appear in Lancaster's historical record because they did not have an uncle, or other relative, to preserve their connection with the local area.

> At least one Lancastrian died on 507 different days during the war – approximately one day in every three for over four years. There were nine days in which ten or more men died and 327 days with only one death.

The second definition of who was killed in the war is simpler but more arbitrary and, strangely, does not necessarily mean killed in the war at all. The war memorial lists all men who died while serving in the military. Most of these were killed at the front, but others were not: Thomas Tite, of 4 Trafalgar Road, Bowerham, died in a training ground accident; Percy Saul, of 9 Springfield Street, died of pneumonia while stationed near Cambridge; George Nicholas Wilkinson, of 34 Aldcliffe Road, was killed by a snake in India and died on 20 April, 1918; and John Hewartson, of 14 Albion Street, was killed by a train near Reading with the 1st/5th while guarding the Great Western Railway. All appear on the memorial, as does the unfortunate Henry Broe of 8 Vincent Street, Primrose, who was 'shot whilst drunk by a friend at Westgate-on-Sea'. Deaths continue to be recorded sometime after the war. The last in the *Reveille* database was Alfred Tyldesley, of 39 Perth Street, who died on 18 August 1921, probably of wounds sustained in July 1916. Most of those who died soon after the war would be included because they died of wounds sustained during the war. In reality men would have continued to die of wounds, and other war-related conditions, for many years afterwards. These deaths are not included because the Imperial War Graves Commission (now the Commonwealth War Graves Commission) used 31 August 1921 as an arbitrary cut-off date for deaths in the war.

While including anyone who died while serving in the military between the outbreak of the War and the end of August 1921 may seem broad, it excludes many people, most obviously civilians. *Reveille* includes one civilian, James Butterworth, who died of grief in 1916 after three of his sons were killed (see Chapter 7). While exceptional, it is unlikely that his was the only death where grief was a contributory factor. Civilians who died in accidents, including the White Lund disaster or industrial diseases are also excluded, a group that would include large numbers of women, as would those killed in accidents and disease brought on by the war.

So who were the 1,055 men who appear as Lancaster's war dead in *Reveille*? Overwhelmingly they were from the army. Some 967 are recorded as being in the army, 97 per cent of those whose service is known. Of the remainder, eighteen were in the Royal Navy, seven in the Royal Marines, four in the Royal Flying Corps and one in the South African Police. This is perhaps unsurprising given Lancaster's importance as an army town. As can be seen from table 5.1, the bulk of the deaths were from the King's Own. As discussed in the previous chapters, the 5th Battalion, which became the 1st/5th, recruited

Deaths by unit and rank

Unit	Deaths
King's Own Royal Lancaster Regiment: Total	425
KORL 1st Battalion	42
KORL 2nd Battalion	27
KORL 1st/4th Battalion	34*
KORL 1st/5th Battalion	198**
KORL 2nd/5th Battalion	48
KORL 8th Battalion	32
Royal Field Artillery	36
Seaforth Highlanders	31
King's Liverpool Regiment	29
Lancashire Fusiliers	29
Border Regiment	25

Table 5.1 **Lancastrian deaths by unit.**
KORL: King's Own Royal Lancaster Regiment. Only units with 25 or more deaths are shown. *includes 2 deaths recorded as 4th Battalion. **includes 14 deaths recorded as 5th Battalion. Within the King's Own: 4 other Lancastrians died with the 3rd Battalion; 3 with the 3rd/5th; 19 with the 6th; 7 with the 7th; and 4 with the 9th. The 7 other deaths are unknown.

heavily from Lancaster and, while the town never had a formal 'Pals' battalion, this unit is the closest to it. As table 5.1 shows, it also had by far the largest number of Lancastrian casualties.

Only 4 per cent of Lancastrians who died were officers, a far lower percentage than for the army as a whole. This perhaps suggests that Lancaster was a strongly working class town and, thus, few officers were recruited. Almost 75 per cent were privates or the equivalent ranks of gunner, sapper, rifleman, guardsman or trooper.

Deaths by date

In popular memory the First World War is associated with large attacks that achieved little except mass casualties. The Battle of the Somme, in the summer and autumn of 1916, is a classic example of this, along with Gallipoli (spring 1915) and Passchendaele (spring 1917). The graph below shows the numbers of Lancastrians killed in each month of the war. It suggests that the Somme did have serious consequences for the town, for July and August 1916 saw 80 deaths in total, but the autumn of 1917 was also bad due, in particular, to the Battle of Cambrai. 1918 saw very heavy casualties due to the German Spring Offensive that was launched by Berlin in an effort to win the war after Russia capitulated, and the subsequent allied Hundred Days offensive in the autumn which finally broke German resistance. The worst period of the war was, however, the spring of 1915 when 121 Lancastrians were killed in around six weeks. This was not, however, due to Gallipoli, but instead was largely due to the almost forgotten Second Battle of Ypres, some of the experiences of which are described in Chapter 4. This battle does not fit the futile attack of popular memory, but instead was a major German attack which saw the first use of gas on the Western Front, although few Lancastrians were killed by it in this attack. Of the Lancastrian deaths at Second Ypres,

Lancastrian deaths by month.

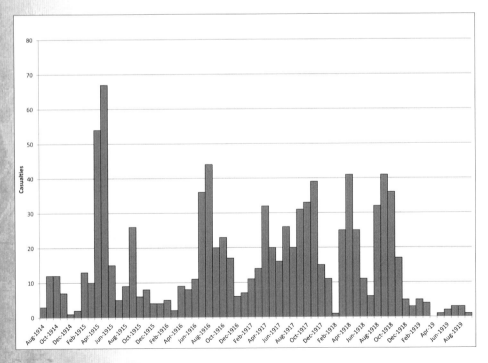

eighty-nine were from the King's Own 1st/5th Battalion with nine more from the 2nd Battalion.

For the 1st/5th this was their first major experience of fighting as they had not long arrived in France. Three days, in particular, stand out as having heavy casualties: 23 and 27 April and 8 May 1915. 23 April was when the battalion was part of the major counterattack, described in Chapter 4, that attempted to push back the initial German breakthrough. It resulted in the deaths of twelve Lancastrians. On 27 April the battalion formed up for another counterattack. This attack was cancelled but the battalion was heavily shelled including one shell that killed thirteen men. Sixteen Lancastrians died that day. 8 May, with nineteen deaths, was the equal worst day of the war for the town although, as we will see below, it was also a lucky day. As described in Chapter 4, the 2nd Battalion had recently relieved the 1st/5th near Frezenburg. On 8 May the Germans overran the 2nd Battalion's positions causing heavy casualties. The 1st/5th was then involved in an unsuccessful counterattack to retake them. In total, nineteen Lancastrians died that day including seven from the 1st/5th and nine from the 2nd. All but one died near Ypres. The other was Henry Botham, from Skerton, who was killed with the Border Regiment at Gallipoli.

According to the Commonwealth War Graves Commission website, over 300 members of 2nd Battalion were killed that day. This shows us two things: that the 2nd Battalion did not recruit heavily from Lancaster as the battalion's 300 dead only included nine Lancastrians; and the decision to withdraw the 1st/5th and replace them with the 2nd was very fortunate for Lancaster as the 1st/5th recruited heavily from the town. Over the period of Second Ypres about 60 per cent of the men killed from the 1st/5th were Lancastrians. Had the 300 casualties taken by the 2nd Battalion been taken by the 1st/5th the city would have had around 200 soldiers killed in a single day rather than the (still horrendous) nineteen it actually experienced. Other towns in north-west England did experience days with casualties of this magnitude, for example Accrington, when the Accrington Pals (11th Battalion, East Lancashire Regiment) suffered 584 casualties

Soldiers of the 1st/5th Battalion, King's Own, with the first issue of gas masks, Belgium, June 1915. (KOM)

killed, wounded or missing on the first day of the Somme, around half of whom are likely to have been from Accrington itself, with many of the remainder from Burnley, Chorley and Blackburn.

September 1915 saw twenty-six Lancastrians killed. Of itself this would be unremarkable given what had happened in the spring and was to happen in many later months, although 25 September again saw nineteen Lancastrians killed on a single day, most of them at the Battle of Loos. Loos does perhaps fit the 'futile attack' memory of the First World War. It was the British Army's first attempt at a major attack which resulted in nearly 60,000 casualties for very limited gains. Twelve of these Lancastrians were from the 8th Battalion of the Seaforth Highlanders: a battalion that lost 502 men at the battle. They were involved in the initial attack on the first day of the assault and suffered casualties on a scale similar to those experienced on the first day of the Somme. Other Lancastrian deaths were in the Cameron Highlanders and the Border and Loyal North Lancashire regiments. Other fighting that day near Ypres killed four other men, three with the King's Shropshire Regiment and one from the Durham Light Infantry. These were probably as a result of subsidiary attacks to support the main Loos offensive. As table 5.1 showed, more Lancastrians died in the Seaforth Highlanders than any other infantry regiment (other than the King's Own). This is because the Seaforth Highlanders put considerable effort into recruiting from towns in northern England, possibly to compensate for the relative lack of population near their own base.

The Battle of the Somme in the summer and autumn of 1916 has come to exemplify the First World War, especially the First Day of the Somme, 1 July, the worst day in the history of the British Army with over 50,000 casualties. As table 5.2 shows, this was a bad period for Lancaster, although the Somme's effects were less severe than Second Ypres and arguably Loos. Lancaster's experience of the Somme was again different from what might be expected given popular narratives of the war. The First Day of the Somme was bad for the town with ten men killed, but the worst day of the campaign was actually 15 August when twelve were killed. The differences between these two days are interesting. Table 5.2 shows that the ten Lancastrians killed on the first day of the Somme came from seven different battalions, six of which took heavy casualties that day. What this shows is that large numbers of battalions went into action that day and took heavy casualties, with the result that Lancastrians spread around

Battalion	Lancastrians killed	Total Killed
1st Battalion King's Own Royal Lancaster Regiment	3	119
1st Battalion King's Own Scottish Borderers	2	125
Tyneside Scottish Battalion, Northumberland Fusiliers	1	161
16th Battalion, Northumberland Fusiliers	1	131
2nd Battalion Border Regiment	1	87
2nd Battalion Yorkshire Regiment	1	66
9th Battalion Cheshire Regiment	1	5

Table 5.2 **The First Day of the Somme: Lancastrians killed by battalion.**
Source: 'Total killed' taken from Commonwealth War Graves Commission website, www.cwgc.org

multiple units were killed. Mercifully for the town, however, the 1st/5th was not involved as it was in reserve near Arras, with the result that Lancaster escaped a fate similar to Accrington's. The 1st Battalion of the King's Own was in action that day and suffered heavy casualties but, thanks to the vagaries of recruiting, only three of these were from Lancaster. By the end of July the 1st/5th had arrived in the Somme sector and the twelve deaths on 15 August were all from this unit. These did not, however, occur in a major attack in the manner of 1 July. Instead, part of the battalion had been ordered to dig trenches near German lines when they came under heavy rifle and machine gun fire which resulted in seventeen deaths and thirty-four men being wounded.

1917 was the worst year of the war for Lancaster with 264 men killed. As the graph above shows, other years saw major peaks in deaths due to battles such as Second Ypres, Loos, the Somme, or the 1918 offensives. By contrast, 1917 was relentless with every month except January having at least ten casualties. The worst month was November with thirty-nine deaths of which fourteen were on the 30th – Lancaster's fourth worst day of the war. This was during the Battle of Cambrai, the first allied offensive in which tanks were extensively used. The 1st/5th's involvement in this battle was again important with eight Lancastrians from the 1st/5th killed on the 30th alone. Seven more Lancastrians died at Cambrai serving with the 1st/4th, all but one on 20 November, the opening day of the battle. As Cambrai started, the Battle of Passchendaele, which had started in July, was drawing to a close. A further eight Lancastrians died in this battle in November, two of whom were from the 2nd/5th which, by then, had changed from being a training battalion to being in active service.

On 21 March 1918, the Germans launched Operation Michael, the first campaign of their Spring Offensive. The offensive was successful in breaking through allied lines and ended the stalemate of trench warfare that had persisted since 1914, leading to desperate allied defence. Eighty-three Lancastrians were killed in this fighting before the end of May. April alone had forty-one casualties making it the fourth equal worst month of the war. After a lull in early summer, the allies launched their own offensive on 8 August. This became known as the Hundred Days Offensive and led to the war ending on 11 November. Again, casualties were high: ninety-six Lancastrians were killed in this fighting, including forty-one in September, making it equal with April for deaths.

Three Lancastrian soldiers died on 6 November 1918: James Booth, of 7 Anne Street; Alfred Morgan, of 45 Aldren's Lane, Skerton; and William Smallshaw, of 26 Bradshaw Street, Primrose. James Booth died of influenza serving in India with the 6th Battalion, King's Own. Alfred Morgan and William Smallshaw were both killed in action in France. They were the last two Lancastrians to be killed in action, although, as described earlier, they were far from the last Lancastrians to die as a result of the war.

Deaths by location

The discussion above points to the worst periods of the war for Lancaster and shows that deaths among men of the town rarely occurred in the stereotypical First World War attack with large numbers of men going 'over the top' in major offensives. Even this account overstates this type of action. During the course of the war there were nine days in which ten or more men from Lancaster died. A total of 125 men died on these days, which tend to be the days that have become significant in popular memory. By contrast, 327 men who were killed, roughly a third of the total, were the only Lancastrian men who died that day. Rather than major offensives killing large numbers of people, this points to a steady stream being killed or dying in a wide range of situations.

One conception of the war that is supported by Lancaster's experience is that, despite being a world war, most deaths took place on the Western Front: 80 per cent of these are found in France or Belgium,

The global nature of the war is evident in the location of the graves of Lancaster's fallen: 501 Lancastrians are buried in France; 307 in Belgium; 99 in the UK; 16 each in Greece and Turkey; and 15 in modern Iraq. Others are buried in (modern-day) Canada, Egypt, Germany, India, Iran, Israel, Italy, Kenya, Malta, the Netherlands, Pakistan, Russia, Syria and Tanzania.

with a further 9 per cent being in the UK. Of these UK graves, seventy-four are in Lancaster: sixty-two in Lancaster Cemetery; and six each in Skerton and Scotforth Cemeteries. The remaining grave and memorial sites are interesting because they again confirm some of our impressions of the war and challenge others. Sixteen soldiers have their grave or memorial in Turkey as a result of the Gallipoli campaign. Sixteen others are found in Greece and fifteen in Iraq as a result of campaigns that have been all but forgotten. The graves in Greece are a result of a campaign to support Greek and Romanian forces in their struggle with Bulgaria. The front line of the Salonika Campaign stretched from Albania to the mouth of the River Struma in Greece. Most of the casualties were from the 2nd or 9th battalions of the King's Own who were involved in the Struma Offensive in August 1916 and the Third Battle of Doiran in September 1918. Most of the Mesopotamian deaths were members of the King's Own's 6th Battalion which had been sent to Basra after Gallipoli. In April 1916 five Lancastrians died in Mesopotamia, probably in the unsuccessful attempt to relieve the siege of Kut-al-Amara. This town, 120 miles south of Baghdad,

Following the 2nd Battalion, King's Own, raid on the Bulgarian lines at Bursuk on the 25 February 1918, a soldier looks after two donkeys and machine gun equipment captured in the raid. (KOM)

Soldiers of the 9th Battalion, King's Own, in Daldi Ravine, Salonika, building a dugout. The terrain is in stark contrast to that experienced by soldiers on the Western Front in France and Belgium. Conditions were far harsher with the winters being very cold and the summers very hot, and many soldiers suffered from disease such as malaria. (KOM)

had been besieged by the Ottomans and finally fell on 29 April with over 13,000 soldiers being taken captive. At the time this was considered to be one of the most humiliating defeats ever suffered by the British Army, although it has since been largely forgotten. Six more Lancastrians died between January and March 1917 in the offensive that captured Baghdad and drove the Ottomans out of southern Mesopotamia.

The picture below shows the grave and memorial sites in northern France and Belgium at which Lancastrians are remembered. The biggest of these sites for Lancastrians is the Menin Gate in Ypres (see also Chapter 8) where 133 Lancastrians are memorialised. The Thiepval Memorial to the Missing of the Somme is second with sixty-two. A straight line between these two sites is 56 miles long, running approximately north to south. In total 606 Lancastrians are buried or memorialised within 10 miles of this line: three-quarters of those killed in France and Belgium; and nearly two-thirds of all Lancastrian casualties. Despite the First World War being a global conflict, for Lancaster at least, much of the dying took place in a remarkably small area. Totalling up the names on graves and memorials, the Ypres area

Grave and memorial sites in France and Belgium (numbers refer to the number of Lancastrians buried or memorialised there).

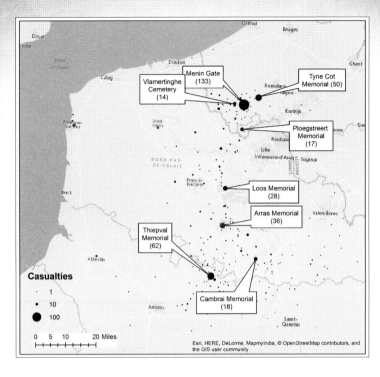

has the largest number of casualties with 307; there are 150 in the Somme area; 91 near Arras; and 51 near Cambrai. These figures underestimate the numbers killed in these places: the grave sites behind the lines and at channel ports show the locations where men, wounded at the front, died of their injuries. More returned to Britain and died there as the number of graves in Lancaster's cemeteries testifies.

Conclusions: Remembering and forgetting

The thing we remember most about the First World War is the large numbers of men in uniform who died. In rightly remembering these men, we tend to overlook the fact that many other people – both men and women – also died in the war who

The Menin Gate Memorial to the Missing (designed by Reginald Blomfeld) was erected to commemorate the missing of the battlefield area of the Ypres Salient. It bears the names of over 54,000 officers and men from the United Kingdom and Commonwealth (except New Zealand and Newfoundland) who fell before 16 August 1917 and have no known grave. When the body of William Butterworth was discovered in 2009 near Lille, his name was removed from the Menin Gate.

were not in uniform. We also tend to assume that the men in uniform died fighting. This is not always the case, for some died in accidents, of disease, or of misadventure.

Popular imagination has a very clear impression of deaths in the First World War, moulded by the first day of the Somme: that of large numbers of men being killed together in huge attacks from one set of trenches to another. Lancaster's experience does little to support this. Most of the men who died were the only men from the town killed that day. Even the major battles tend not to conform to this stereotype. Lancaster's worst experience was the Second Battle of Ypres: a defensive battle which has been largely forgotten. At the Somme, the worst experience was on 15 August 1916 in an operation to dig trenches, rather than 1 July. The spring and autumn of 1918 saw mass casualties, but by this point the war had become far more mobile than the trench warfare that we tend to remember. The deaths away from the Western Front follow the same pattern. Roughly the same number of Lancastrians died in Turkey (Gallipoli), Mesopotamia and Greece. The Gallipoli campaign is seared in popular memory while the Greek and, at least until recently, Mesopotamian campaigns had been almost completely forgotten. There is, of course, a significant amount of luck in the odds of death. Around 40 per cent of Lancastrians killed were in the King's Own, and nearly half of these were in its 1st/5th Battalion; the locations of these units at crucial moments would have a major impact on the pattern of casualties. Nevertheless, this does indicate that the First World War was a far more complex event than we tend to remember and our memories and histories of it tend to be very selective, focusing on some stories and forgetting others. Focussing on one town's experience reveals this complexity.

JOHN WELCH
(1884-1966)

With the emphasis on mass death, it is easy to forget the men who came home from the war. The King's Own Royal Regiment Museum holds papers of some such men. John Welch, for example, was a Lancaster solicitor. Having joined the Officer Training Corps in January 1915, he was commissioned as 2nd Lieutenant 4th (T.) Battalion King's Own Royal Lancaster Regiment, June 13, 1915, and promoted to captain in July 1917. His bills, receipts and letters suggest the challenges of an officer seeking to be appropriately clad and shod, equipped, transported, fed and watered. In January 1916 he went shopping for military supplies, purchasing a lamp, a torch, a battery, a bulb, a trench dagger, a water sterilizer, a revolver lanyard, a steel mirror, a sleeping bag, a tabloid case, a waterproof wallet, a cooker, a water bucket and a skin waistcoat. He also looked after his men: in October 1915, for example, buying 'drinks and smokes for the troops'.

He served in France from January to August 1916, and again from May 1917 to April 1919. He was wounded during the Battle of the Somme on 8 August 1916; the King's Own Regiment Museum holding equipment labels on which 'deceased officer's kit' has been amended to 'wounded'. His letters to his aunt at home reveal a powerful use of understatement: 'It is rather disconcerting to be talking to a man who suddenly shows you the bottom of his boots' (22 December 1916).

A solicitor, John Welch retired early to pursue his community interests and became a county councillor. As Chairman of the Lancashire Education Committee he was very committed to education at both school and university level. His supporting role in the establishment of the new Lancaster University in 1964 is commemorated by the 'John Welch Room' at the University. He married Margaret Flora Joy Lane in 1925 and had two children. His family recalls that, although he recovered from his physical injuries, he had nightmares from time to time for the rest of his life and would never talk about the war. His post-war life reminds us of the potential of the lives lost to war.

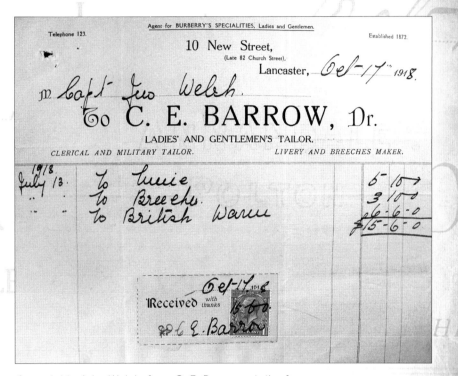

A receipt to John Welch, from C. E. Barrow, a tailor for many years on New Street, only recently closed. For 'tunic, breeches and British Warm'. (KOM)

6

THE MEN WHO DID NOT FIGHT

Although most Britons supported their country's entry into the First World War, there was no shortage of voices opposing the conflict. Many members of the Independent Labour Party criticised Britain's involvement. So too did most Quakers, along with some Baptists and Methodists, as well as a few members of the Church of England. Some critics of the war believed that ordinary people had no stake in a conflict being fought to defend the financial interests of the rich and powerful. Others suggested that killing on the battlefield could never be reconciled with the Christian command to 'love thy neighbour as thyself'. Such arguments were often combined, perhaps no matter for surprise, given that the development of socialism in Britain had been shaped as much by Methodism as Marx.

Lancaster did not have a strong tradition of labour radicalism before the First World War. No Labour candidate stood for election in the town until 1922, when the Party's unsuccessful candidate was Fenner Brockway, who had after 1914 been a prominent opponent of the war and founder of the No-Conscription Fellowship. Some of Britain's big industrial cities witnessed considerable industrial unrest after 1914, often fuelled by resentment over poor working conditions and long hours, which were an inevitable consequence of the need to keep supplies flowing to the army. The potential impact of the conflict on Lancaster's economy certainly raised fears during the early days of the war that mass unemployment could lead to suffering and poverty. In the event, the economic impact proved to be less

An interior view of the National Filling Factory: women weighing explosives for the shells. (LCM)

severe than anticipated, in large part due to the rapid growth of the munitions industry.

The conditions faced by the mainly female workforce in some munitions factories were often very poor. The massive explosion at White Lund in 1917 showed the perils of working in armaments production, even though just ten people died, but the real dangers could be more insidious. Sixteen-year-old Isabella Clarke, who worked at White Lund, later recalled how one of her friends died from the toxic effects of loading 9.2in shells with gas. Despite the poor conditions, serious labour unrest was rare in Lancaster, although in spring 1916 thirty men left their work in a shipbreaking yard in neighbouring Morecambe, in breach of the Munitions of War Act. They soon returned, though, when told by a local solicitor that their action was illegal. *The Lancaster Observer* praised the men for their common sense, contrasting their behaviour with that of workers in some other towns and cities, where protests often took on a more militant character.

Conscientious Objectors

Few people in Lancaster publicly questioned whether Britain was right to go to war in the summer of 1914. Although the town's response to news of the conflict was muted, the public mood was not one calculated to encourage open expressions of outright dissent. As soldiers departed for the Front, and the casualty lists mounted, any expression of disagreement with the war could easily be seen as unpatriotic at a time of national crisis.

The recruitment campaigns that took place in Lancaster throughout 1915 were calculated to bring social pressure to bear on all those who had not already enlisted. It was nevertheless still possible for men who did not want to fight to continue with their normal peacetime occupation (although the introduction of the Derby Scheme in the autumn of 1915 increased the pressure). The passing of the Military Service Act in January 1916 transformed the situation. The introduction of conscription was bound to prove controversial for many in Britain, given the lack of a tradition of compulsory military service, although only one minister, Sir John Simon, resigned from the Cabinet in protest. The Act provided the foundation for the conscription of younger unmarried men, and established a series of Military Service Tribunals to hear appeals from those who believed they should not be called up, typically on the grounds of domestic hardship or because they were engaged in work of national importance. But – after considerable debate in Parliament – the government also agreed on a clause that would allow men to appeal against military service on the grounds of conscience. Men who believed they should be exempted from joining the army, for whatever reason, had to fill out an exemption form before their case was heard by one of the tribunals.

Around 17,000 men from across Britain eventually became conscientious objectors. Most agreed to undertake some form of alternative service, perhaps entering the Royal Army Medical Corps, or joining the Friends Ambulance Unit (founded by Quakers although formally independent from the Society of Friends). A few thousand 'absolutists' refused to carry out any

SECTION III.—APPLICATIONS FOR CERTIFICATES OF EXEMPTION MADE BY OR IN RESPECT OF MEN UNDER SECTION 2 (1) OF THE ACT.

1. An application may be made by or in respect of a man for a certificate of exemption from the provisions of the Act on any of the following grounds :—

(*a*) On the ground that it is expedient in the national interests that the man should, instead of being employed in military service, be engaged in other work in which he is habitually engaged ; or

(*b*) On the ground that it is expedient in the national interests that the man should, instead of being employed in military service, be engaged in other work in which he wishes to be engaged ; or

(*c*) If the man is being educated or trained for any work, on the ground that it is expedient in the national interests that, instead of being employed in military service, he should continue to be so educated or trained ; or

(*d*) On the ground that serious hardship would ensue, if the man were called up for Army service, owing to his exceptional financial or business obligations or domestic position ; or

(*e*) On the ground of ill-health or infirmity ; or

(*f*) On the ground of a conscientious objection to the undertaking of combatant service ;

and the Local Tribunal, if they consider the grounds of the application established, shall issue such a certificate to the man in respect of whom the application is made.

The Military Service Act allowed for possible grounds for exemption. (MJH)

work that could be seen as supporting the war effort and were often imprisoned as a result. Some were handed over to the military, where they often faced court-martial, and a few were even threatened with execution for refusing to obey orders. The county of Lancashire produced nearly 2,000 conscientious objectors. Most came from the large urban areas in the south of the country. Surprisingly few came from the towns of Lancaster and Morecambe, though a significant number did come from the villages that stretched up the Lune Valley. The surviving records give a fascinating insight both into the way the local tribunals operated and the attitudes of the men who appeared before them.

Only a small number of men who appeared before tribunals in Lancaster and the surrounding areas sought exemption on grounds of conscience. This may in part have been because they believed they were more likely to be successful if they claimed to be doing work of national importance. It may also have been that they were fearful of the hostile reaction to conscientious objectors across Britain. Some editorial notes that appeared in the *Lancaster Observer* towards the end of February 1916 give a good sense of the hostility of local opinion towards conscientious objectors.

THE MEN WHO WOULD NOT GO TO WAR

It is easy to understand the fears both of those who went to war and the families they left behind. It is important to remember, too, that the departure of thousands of men for the Front created enormous economic disruption at home. The situation was particularly acute for small businesses. In September 1916, the Lancaster Borough Tribunal heard appeals on behalf of a number of young men employed in local building and joinery businesses, which found it almost impossible to operate without skilled labour. The same Tribunal also heard an appeal from a 'basketmaker' who promised to teach his craft to others if he was allowed to remain at home. The results of such cases were not always predictable. Many men were ordered to join up as soon as possible, even if it would bring hardship to their family, but others, like a Lancaster piano builder, were for some reason given exemption.

Among the businesses hardest hit by the introduction of conscription in 1916 were family farms. The tribunals often reacted sceptically to claims that agricultural work would be disrupted if the younger men were sent into the army. This may have reflected the fact that some tribunal members did not really understand farming. It may also have been that they suspected farmers were trying to protect their sons from having to fight. This was sometimes true. One farmer who worked land in the Lune Valley dismissed his paid workers so that he could claim his own sons were indispensible to his business. The reluctance of farming families to free up labour for the war effort created considerable resentment in Lancaster. The town's civil leaders repeatedly called on the local villages to follow the example of their urban neighbours by sending as many men as possible into the army.

R.—41 **MILITARY SERVICE ACTS, 1916.**

*Name of Tribunal*_____   *Number of Case*_____

APPLICATION AS TO EXEMPTION.

(The attached duplicate must also be filled up by the Applicant.)

Any person making a false statement or false representation is liable to imprisonment.

1. Man in respect of whom application made :—

    (*a*) Name (*in full*)

    (*b*) Age last birthday   Date of birthday

    (*c*) Married or single   If married, date of marriage

    (*d*) Address (*in full*)

    (*e*) Address at date of National Registration
       (15th August, 1915)

    (*f*) Occupation, profession or business (*Give full and exact details*)

2. Whether engaged in the same or a similar occupation before 15th August, 1915.
    If so engaged, (*a*) The precise occupation

    (*b*) How long employed in the occupation before 15th August, 1915

    (*c*) Name and address of last employer when so employed before that date

    (*a*) Name of present employer, if any

    (*b*) Address (*in full*) ...   .

    (*c*) Business ...   .

4. Ground on which application is made. [*See footnote on back of duplicate. It will be sufficient if the letter* (a), (b), (c), (d), (e), (f) *or* (g) (*whichever is appropriate*), *is entered.*]

5. Nature of application. (*A certificate of exemption may be absolute, conditional or temporary. Also, a certificate granted on conscientious grounds may be for exemption from combatant service only, or may be conditional on the applicant being engaged in some work which, in the opinion of the Tribunal, is of national importance.*)

(80750) Wt. 9976—28 75M 8/16 H & S   [P.T.O.

A sample blank exemption form. (MJH)

The local newspapers reported on the deliberations of the Military Service Tribunals. (MJH)

TRIBUNALS AT WORK.

SITTINGS OF THE BOROUGH AND RURAL COURTS.

THE CORPORATION CRITICISED.

MORECAMBE AND KIRKBY LONSDALE TRIBUNALS.

The paper noted that 'Only men can defeat our malignant foe … Neither religious scruples, nor business exigencies, nor parental ties afford the excuse for standing back while others do the work.' It went on to suggest that any who sought exemption on whatever grounds 'will be social lepers, abhorred and abused as cowards'. Men who appealed to the tribunals for exemption from military service on grounds of conscience knew that they were unlikely to be treated with much sympathy.

The challenges likely to face would-be conscientious objectors became clear on 8 March 1916, when the Lunesdale Tribunal first met in the village of Hornby, a few miles north-east of Lancaster. Among the large number of claims for exemption from military service were ten from conscientious objectors. Three brothers from one farming family sought exemption on the grounds that killing another human being was contrary to their beliefs. Their case attracted a good deal of national attention when it transpired their father was actually a tribunal member! One applicant was asked whether he would defend his girlfriend if a German soldier 'threw her down, and attempted to ravish her'. Another was told to explain how he would react if he saw 'a German crucifying a child on a door' (reports of such things happening in Belgium had long circulated in the British press). A third was quizzed about his actions should he witness his mother being killed. When the men before the Tribunal responded uncertainly to such questions, or denied outright that they would ever use force, the Tribunal Chairman roundly condemned them for lack of patriotism: 'How a man can talk this rubbish you conscientious objectors put before us I don't know.' The contemptuous tone of the questioning was serious enough to be raised in Parliament shortly after.

A few days later, it was the turn of the Lancaster Borough Tribunal to hear appeals from men who objected to conscription on grounds of conscience. The first man to be heard was 23-year-old Norman Witham, a cashier in a local bank, who presented a long document setting out his belief in 'the brotherhood of man'. His case was not helped by the fact that he was a Wesleyan Methodist – the Wesleyans generally supported the war, although a local Minister was Honourable Secretary of the Lancaster branch of the No-Conscription Fellowship – and Witham was closely questioned by the Chairman and the Military Representative about his understanding of the New Testament. He was also asked whether he would act to defend his sister if she were attacked. The case of Witham was followed by a number of others, including a schoolteacher who said that war was contrary to 'religion and humanity', and another young Wesleyan who argued that war represented a 'denial of Christianity'. A 38-year-old 'artist-designer' said that he thought war was 'of the devil' but acknowledged he attended no church or chapel. Much of the questioning was tinged with sarcasm. The Military Representative noted scathingly to one applicant that 'You can train your conscience … to do almost anything'. Many cases were nevertheless accepted, and the applicants were given exemption from combatant service (and typically required to carry out work of national importance or join an organisation like the Friends Ambulance Unit). A few were not so lucky. The press report of the Tribunal hearing ends with a laconic statement that 'Later, a painter (24) applied for exemption on the grounds that he strongly objected to killing, but the application was refused.'

The tribunals in and around Lancaster continued to be busy over the next few months. In April, the Lonsdale Appeal Tribunal – which heard appeals from the local tribunals – met at Lancaster Castle to hear numerous cases including those of a number of conscientious objectors.

Most men who sought exemption did so because of the hardship it would cause their employers or families, but a small number refused to fight on grounds of conscience. Many conscientious objectors were ready to undertake some kind of alternative work. A few were not and were sent to prison. Although Lancashire produced a large number of conscientious objectors, only a small number came from the town of Lancaster itself.

The case of a 23-year-old cashier at a local bank, reported in the Lancaster Observer *on 17 March 1916, offers an example of the moral and religious reasoning presented to the tribunal. (MJH)*

CONSCIENTIOUS OBJECTORS.

Ten or a dozen applicants applied for exemption on moral and religious grounds, and for a short time the proceedings were animated. The spectators included several ministers.

A cashier and general clerk in a local bank, 23 years of age, applied for exemption on religious and moral grounds. He had attached a long written document to his application form, which he said set forth his views. The Chairman read the document, which set forth that applicant took his stand on obedience to Christ, who was tempted to make use of the powers of the world to bring about His Kingdom, but steadfastly refused. He declined to accept the kingdoms of this world and the glory of them at the offer of the Tempter.

"Do you want any more of this reading," asked the Chairman of the other members of the tribunal, adding "There is a lot of it."

Assent being expressed the Chairman proceeded with the reading. Applicant set forth that his understanding of the Word of God was that kingdoms were not to be established by force or militarism. Christ showed that the world was to be overcome not by violence but by unfailing love, and as a follower of Christ he (applicant) was bound to recognise that force was no remedy for evil. The Fatherhood of God involved the brotherhood of man, and holding that view he could not countenance war. Some things were of more importance than empire, one of which was obedience to conscience.

One case was refused altogether. Other conscientious objectors were given non-combatant service, though often only after suffering harsh remarks that they preferred 'a comfortable occupation at home', with the clear hint that they were using claims of conscience simply to avoid danger. Some of the men were reprimanded for making speeches rather than giving evidence (tribunal members seldom looked kindly on those who sought to turn the proceedings into a debating chamber). Many were asked the familiar question about whether they would use force to protect family members – and if so how they could justify seeking exemption from military service. The cases before the Lonsdale Tribunal show that conscientious objectors continued to be drawn disproportion-ately from rural areas outside Lancaster. Voluntary enlistment in north Lancashire had been lower in the villages throughout 1914 and 1915, probably because it was so difficult to spare young men from small family farms. The recruiting rallies that had taken place in the bigger towns in any case seemed remote in rural areas where transport was poor and the communities close-knit. Religious observance was also higher in the countryside. When conscription was introduced, it was always likely that many conscientious objectors would come from the countryside, rather than from Lancaster with its strong military presence.

Henry Alty, a joiner from Pilling near Lancaster, faced a court martial for refusing to fight. His case was raised in Parliament, where it was claimed that he had been ill-treated, 'prodded behind with a sharp instrument until he collapsed on the floor, and ... was then dragged some considerable distance and afterwards thrown on top of the barrow.'

Young men who belonged to the Society of Friends generally found it straightforward to persuade tribunals to offer them exemption from combatant service given that the Quaker views on war were well-known. Most Quakers, like 32-year-old Joseph Muschamp, an undertaker who lived on Denmark Street, claimed absolute exemption from military service, but were only offered conditional exemption, typically requiring them to serve with the Friends Ambulance Unit. The Quakers who really fell foul of the Military Service Act were those who refused to undertake any kind of work that could be seen as supporting the war effort. The experiences of the two Walmesley brothers, Cyril and Alwyne, who were educated in Lancaster and later at a Quaker boarding school, illustrates how the treatment of a conscientious objector varied according to the kind of exemption they sought. Cyril joined a Friends War Victim Relief Committee unit in 1915, before the Military Service Act was introduced, and when his case was heard in absentia in February 1916 he was given exemption from combatant service on the grounds that he was already doing valuable work. He was later praised in the *Lancaster Guardian* for 'doing very efficient work in repairing a hospital damaged by the German bombardment' while 'living in considerable danger'.

The case of Alwyne Walmesley was very different. Alwyne was teaching in Cambridge when he appeared before the local tribunal there, which gave him exemption from combatant service, but required him to join the Friends Ambulance Unit (FAU). A few months later he asked for the case to be reopened, resigning from the Unit citing grounds of conscience, but the authorities refused to reconsider his position. He was subsequently arrested in Lancaster in the summer of 1917, and brought before the local Bench, where he claimed that the FAU was, despite its humanitarian ethos, still a military service. He was sentenced to six months hard labour in Wormwood Scrubs.

The regime in Wormwood Scrubs was notoriously harsh. Some conscientious objectors imprisoned there later recalled that they often contemplated suicide. Although Alwyne's objections to serving with the FAU were accepted as genuine when he appeared before a tribunal held at the prison, he was once again arrested following his release early in 1918, telling the Court in Lancaster that his views had become still firmer during his time in prison. Alwyne was taken to Park Hall Camp near Oswestry, where he faced a court martial, at which he repeated his claim that only a reinvigoration of the 'spiritual life of the individual' could prevent civilisation 'from plunging into that anarchy to which it is clearly advancing'. He was throughout his long ordeal astonishingly resilient. He praised the chaplains who ministered to prisoners at the Scrubs, and while at Oswestry recalled his time

Spencer Ellwood Barrow was an architect and honorary treasurer of the Royal Lancaster Infirmary (RLI). Although he was a member of the Society of Friends, he enlisted in September 1914 as he felt that facing German aggression was more important than his religious beliefs. He died on 16 November 1915 from wounds received in action in May 1915 at Frezenberg. He is buried in Scotforth Cemetery and there is a memorial window to him in the RLI.

in prison in London as 'in a peculiar sense a happy period … the only punishment is the want of self-expression and the feeling of the utter stupidity and wastefulness of the whole process.'

The names of conscientious objectors who appeared before the tribunals were not usually recorded in the published proceedings, meaning that it is sometimes hard to identify individuals, although recent research has made it possible to identify a number of them. Almost all conscientious objectors who appeared before tribunals in Lancaster and the surrounding villages based their claim on their religious views (though in Lancaster itself a significant number acknowledged that they did not regularly attend Church or Chapel). As well as Quakers, there were Wesleyans and Primitive Methodists, Baptists and Congregationalists. A rather different attitude towards conscription was in evidence at the Conference of the Miners Federation of Great Britain, which met in Lancaster a few weeks after the passing of the Military Service Act. The delegates passed a motion opposing 'the spirit of conscription', and expressed determination to prevent any extension to the groups of men eligible for call-up. They also discussed whether to begin 'agitation' for the Act's repeal. The idea that the First World War was being fought with the blood of the workers was not uncommon in Britain, even if it was seldom heard at the tribunals that met in and around Lancaster, where labour militancy was traditionally lower than in the big cities of south Lancashire.

Occupational Exemptions

Most men who sought certificates of exemption from the tribunals were not conscientious objectors. They instead sought exemption on other grounds, most often claiming that recruitment into the army would take them away from work of national importance, or leave their family destitute. Such claims were scrutinised carefully by the tribunals, and often turned down, much to the disgust of the applicants. The rate of rejection became higher as the war progressed, and the need for soldiers greater than ever, and few claimants ever gained more than a few weeks' grace to put their affairs in order. The tribunals in and around Lancaster closely interrogated those seeking exemption. Although the tone of the questioning was seldom as harsh as it was with conscientious objectors, many tribunal members clearly believed that most men seeking to avoid military service were motivated by a desire to put their private interest over the good of their country.

Some of the claims that came before the tribunals received particularly short shrift. The Lancaster Borough Tribunal that met in early May 1916 considered a request from a local hairdresser for an extension to his certificate of exemption, which had been issued some weeks earlier, in order to allow him to put his affairs in order before joining up. He told the Tribunal that several munitions factories had opened near his premises, and asked what was to be done for the workers who crowded his shop. The Military Representative tersely replied that 'we must all grow beards'. At the same Tribunal, a clogger argued in vain that his work was of national importance, given that many poorer residents could not afford expensive leather shoes. A local baker argued without success that his son should be allowed to continue working in the business since he did much of the lifting and carrying.

Many claims for exemption on grounds of work of national priority came from farmers in the countryside around Lancaster. One farmer sought exemption for his two sons on the grounds that he needed them to work the land, but was told he could keep just one of them at home ('It's cruel,' a member of the public called out). The Lancaster Rural District Tribunal heard a particularly large number of cases. Many farmers described at length how they could not get labour to cover for sons called up for service. The results varied from case to case, but in general only a temporary exemption was offered, in order to allow the farmer to find other labour. The fact that so many appeals for exemption came from men who worked in the family business meant that tribunal members often suspected that emotion rather than the needs of the farm was the real motive behind an application for exemption. Nor were they generally sympathetic to those who said their business would be ruined. Although most claimants who came before the tribunals did not argue that war was wrong, or that they objected to taking a human life, many of them were in effect dissenting from the state's claim that it had the right to mobilise the population for total war. Such sentiments were unlikely to find favour at a time of total war.

Many claims for exemption were sponsored by major businesses in Lancaster. In March 1916, the works manager at Waring and Gillow, which had by now been converted from manufacturing fine furniture to building aircraft wings, was ordered to appear before the Lancaster Borough Tribunal to explain why the company laid off older men but kept on younger men who would otherwise be eligible for military service. The Tribunal accepted the explanation that the firm needed to keep its 'best men' in order to operate efficiently, but made it clear that the company should whenever possible release younger men. Lord Ashton also protested vigorously from time to time against demands that more of his workers should be sent into the forces, pointing out that his factories would then be forced to close, putting thousands of women and older men out of work. Lancaster Borough Council similarly sought exemption for large numbers of employees, a move that caused some embarrassment for councillors who sat on the tribunals. Leaders of these organisations were naturally careful to pronounce their support for the war effort (businessmen like Ashton had indeed been vocal in encouraging their workers to enlist during the years of voluntary recruitment). But they were also intensely aware of the financial and operational consequences of conscription for their businesses as it shrunk the workforce still further. The introduction of conscription was not only a challenge for those whose consciences led them to refuse to take up arms.

There were of course many other ways in which individuals could behave in a way that disrupted the war effort, though this was most often the result of putting personal interests ahead of the wider national interest, rather than a deliberate act of dissent.

The Munitions Tribunal in Lancaster met regularly to hear the case of workers whose behaviour could undermine the effectiveness of local munitions factories. One tribunal session held early in 1918 heard cases ranging from gambling to falling asleep 'on the job'. Other sessions heard cases concerning absenteeism or rowdy behaviour. The regular military tribunals often expressed irritation that many young men were 'sheltering' in munitions factories, enjoying well-paid employment, rather than joining the army (a strategy that some men certainly followed). The local police in Lancaster also had to deal with soldiers who went AWOL, either in a deliberate attempt to escape the rigours of military life, or as a consequence of too much alcohol. Some Lancastrians were brought before the Bench for hoarding food. Farmers were prosecuted for refusing to comply with instructions from the War Agricultural Committee. Such examples of anti-social behaviour received considerable censure in the local press. The *Lancaster Observer* vented its spleen against a cyclist who, when stopped for riding without a front light, said that he was a munitions worker and would deliberately stay away from work in protest. The magistrates took a predictably unsympathetic view of his behaviour when deciding on the appropriate penalty.

The Stone of Remembrance in Tavistock Gardens, London, was unveiled in 1994. (CPB)

Conclusions

North Lancashire was not a hotbed of conscientious objectors. The town's proud military heritage probably created social pressure that made it hard for young men to refuse to fight. Nor did the tribunals in Lancaster and the surrounding areas behave with particular harshness. 'Conchies' were treated with disdain rather than cruelty. Yet it did take a particular kind of courage to refuse to join up. It is still not clear exactly how many men from Lancaster and the surrounding towns and cities refused to undertake combatant service. The reports in the local press suggest that there were probably a greater number of conscientious objectors than is realised today. Most of these men have faded from history – although there is now a memorial to them in London. Their experiences, like those of the soldiers who fought in the trenches of France, form part of the human tapestry changed forever by the First World War.

7

Lancaster's Lost: The Impact of the Deaths at Home

Chapters 4 and 5 described some of the times, places and events in which Lancastrians fought. The men who died were not just soldiers, sailors and airmen, they were also people who lived, worked and played in the town – and 'loved and were loved', to quote John McRae's poem, 'In Flanders Fields'. This chapter is based primarily on information about the 1,055 Lancastrians who died in uniform, as listed in *Reveille*. This does not provide a perfect definition of every Lancastrian who died as a result of the war, but we are lucky to have as it does provide a comprehensive record of 'the men of Lancaster' who died in uniform during the war and in its immediate aftermath. This chapter uses this information in an attempt to understand what the losses from the First World War meant to Lancaster.

Family tragedies

In 1914 the Cathcart family, John and Mary, and their three children Annie, George and James, lived at 97 Dale Street. They had not long moved to the house; the 1911 Census records them as living on Cable Street (misnaming them as 'Catheart'). On 6 September 1914, perhaps inspired by the 'Gallant 200' (see Chapter 1), James and George Cathcart went to join up. They probably queued up together, perhaps with a friend, as their service numbers were 2091 and 2093 respectively, and they enlisted into the 1st/5th Battalion of the King's Own Royal

97 Dale Street (the middle door), home of the Cathcart family. (ING)

The Cathcart brothers' names on the city's war memorial. (ING)

Lancaster Regiment. As described in Chapter 4, the battalion sailed to France on 15 February 1915 and marched into Ypres on 9 April. This placed them in the way of the German offensive at the Second Battle of Ypres which began on 22 April. George was killed the following day, along with twelve other Lancastrians, in the counterattack that unsuccessfully tried to push back the German advance. His obituary in the *Lancaster Observer* notes that James was advancing with him when he was lost. By the time this obituary appeared on 7 May, James was also dead. He had been killed on 4 May, along with six other Lancastrians from the 1st/5th in the shelling that led up to the

125

German assault on Frezenburg. They were 19 and 17 years old respectively when they died.

The Cathcarts' tragedy is hardly unique, and indeed by the standards of the time it is barely remarkable. When John Adams was killed alongside George Cathcart on 23 April 1915, his family had already lost their oldest son, Charles, in 1914, while a third son, Henry, died exactly one year after Charles on 26 September 1915 at the Battle of Loos. Their parents lived at 4 Winders Court, Monmouth Street, an area between Moor Lane and Nelson Street where the housing has today been replaced by car parks. The Dinsdales of 34 Havelock Street, Bowerham also lost three sons, William, Frank and George, before the end of 1915. In 1917 the Gardners, who lived nearby at 13 Bowerham Terrace, lost Reginald on 9 April, Alfred on 10 October and, less than a month later, James, on 2 November. James was not even posted overseas but was in a Training Reserve Battalion. He is buried in Lancaster Cemetery. The Williams of Hamner Place, Bowerham and the Glovers of 1 Piccadilly, Scotforth also lost three sons. The Butterworth family of 27 Green Street, Bulk fared even worse. William Butterworth was killed on 18 October 1914, followed by Christopher on 8 May 1915 serving with the 2nd Battalion, King's Own, at Frezenburg, and Hugh with the 1st/5th three months later. On 12 August 1916 their father, James, was reported in the *Lancaster Guardian* to have 'died from debility, caused by having three sons killed and two severely wounded in the war.' A fourth son, John, subsequently died on 23 June 1917. He may have been one of the severely wounded brothers as he is buried in Lancaster Cemetery.

Fred Carr, 24 Alfred Street, was killed on 22 April 1915. He had six children. Thomas Slater, 11 Main Street, Skerton was killed the following day. He had five children.

In total, 134 of the dead in *Reveille* are listed as brothers, 13 per cent of the total Lancastrians killed. Even this is not all of them. The two Corless brothers are not marked as such on the memorial, which lists five men named Corless. Bryant Browning, of 1 Marton Street, was killed on the first day of the Somme with the 1st Battalion, King's Own. His brother, Arthur was killed the following day, also on the Somme, but is not recorded as a

Lancastrian as their family home was at 22 Beach Street, Bare and he thus appears on Morecambe War Memorial.

Deaths by age

These are only eight of the families who lost sons during the war. It is difficult to understand what the loss of around 1,055 mainly young men in a very few years would have meant for a town the size of Lancaster. The 1911 Census records Lancaster Municipal Borough as having a population of 41,410 of whom 20,204 were male. This suggests that 2.6 per cent of the town's total population, or 5.2 per cent of the male population, were killed (these numbers must be taken with a little caution as they assume that all of the Lancastrians included in *Reveille* were also enumerated in the 1911 Census.) Deaths in the war, however, had a very distinct age profile as shown in the graph below. The average age of death among Lancastrians was 26.6 but the most common, by some way, was only 19. Eighty-four per cent of those who died were between 18 and 34. The figures on age of death are

Numbers of Lancastrians killed, by age. These figures are based on the 638 casualties we have ages for – 60.4 per cent of the total deaths. (Source: Reveille)

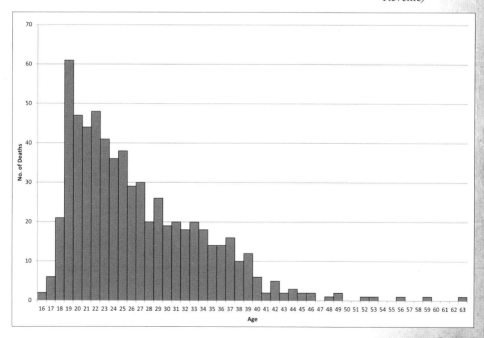

Name	Address	Unit	Date of Death	Circumstances of death	Age	Enlisted
Matthew Farrell	6 Little John St.	1st/5th Bn. KORL	14/4/15	2nd Ypres	16	Before the War
Harry Grice	7 Ripley St & 20 Railway St.	1st/5th Bn. KORL	27/4/15	2nd Ypres	16	Aug 1914
James Cathcart	97 Dale St.	1st/5th Bn. KORL	4/5/15	2nd Ypres	17	Sept 1914
Stanley Bates		1st/5th Bn. KORL	9/5/15	2nd Ypres	17	Aug 1914
John Mount	112 North Edward St.	2nd Bn. Royal Fusiliers	17/1/16	Died of dysentery, Lancaster	17	Jan 1915
William Ritchie	42 Avondale Rd.	1st/5th Bn. KORL	25/6/16	Killed in action near Arras	17	Sept 1915
William Stephenson	43 Ulster Rd	Royal Field Artillery	21/10/16	Gassed during the Somme	17	April 1915
John Hewartson		2nd Bn. KORL	31/10/16	Killed in action, Greece	17	Unknown

Table 7.1 **16 and 17 year olds killed.**
Abbreviations: KORL: King's Own Royal Lancaster Regiment; Battalion. (Source: *Reveille*)

based on the 638 records which list age at death. These constitute 60.4 per cent of the total and can be considered representative. A little estimation using census data suggests that 15 per cent of Lancastrian males born between 1886 and 1899 were killed, peaking at 20 per cent of those born in 1895. Records from the 1st/5th, suggest for every man killed, three were wounded which suggests that only around 20 per cent of men born in 1895 survived the war unscathed and over half of the cohort born between 1886 and 1899 were killed or injured.

The above table details the eight Lancastrians killed under the age of eighteen. Although there are frequent stories of boys who lied about their age to join up, this does not seem to have happened in Lancaster, at least not with fatal results. Instead, most of the very young who were killed were either associated with the Territorials before the war, or joined up immediately on its outbreak. As a result, many were in the 1st/5th Battalion and so four of the eight were killed at the Second Battle of Ypres. The remainder died in 1916. It appears, therefore, that as the pressure on manpower increased, leading to the introduction of conscription in 1916, and perhaps as the full horror of modern warfare became apparent, the military actually got better at keeping the very young out of harm's way. It is also interesting to note that casualties among the very young came from across the social spectrum. Matthew Farrell lived with his mother on Little John Street, now an alley off Church Street near the Stonewell pub which at the time would have had very low-quality housing. His father had left many years before suggesting the family was very poor. Stanley Bates was, by contrast, probably from a wealthy family. He had been a cadet at Lancaster Royal Grammar School and was gazetted at the outbreak of war, being promoted to become the youngest full lieutenant in the British Army. His father, the second in command of the 1st/5th, had been invalided home a few days before Stanley was killed.

The oldest deaths were among men who, although in uniform and thus recorded as war deaths, served at home. The oldest was Henry Tripp, aged 63. We know little about him other than he lived at 55 Norfolk Street, Skerton, and was a private in the 3rd (Special Reserve) Battalion, King's Own, a training unit that did not serve overseas. He died on 2 July 1916 and is buried in Skerton Cemetery. Major C.J. Holmes was the Surgeon Major at Bowerham Barracks and lived at 50 Regent Street. He died of illness aged 59 in April 1916. Thomas Tite had served, and been decorated, during the Boer War but had since retired. He lived in Trafalgar Road, Bowerham, and rejoined the military at the outbreak of war as an instructor. A training ground

Private Matthew Farrell (right) at a pre-war 5th Battalion Territorial Force annual camp. He was killed in action on 13 April 1915 aged 16. (KOM)

Seventy per cent of Lancastrians killed in the War were under 30 years old. From a national perspective, the highest increases in mortality rates (as compared with those that could be expected within a population not at war) were for men aged 19–24.

accident resulted in his death in January 1916, aged 56. Holmes and Tite are both buried in Lancaster Cemetery.

The evidence for who was the oldest soldier to be killed in action is slightly contradictory. Ernest Harlowe of 8 Havelock Street, Bowerham, was killed in action on 27 May 1915 near Ypres. He is recorded by the Commonwealth War Graves Commission as being 46 but his obituary in the *Lancaster Observer* records him as only being 42. William Warwick of 14 Primrose Street died of wounds on 14 May 1916 aged 45. He was a member of the West Yorkshire Regiment's 1st Garrison Battalion and is buried at Etaples Military Cemetery. Etaples was a major military camp with several hospitals and it is unclear whether his injuries were sustained at the front or on base duties. William Johnson of 14 Sun Street was 44 when he died in February 1915. Although he is reported killed in action, he is buried at Longuenesse (St Omer) Souvenir Cemetery well behind the front lines, which is unusual for someone killed in action. Two 43-year-olds definitely did die in action: John Pye, of 37 Marton Street, killed with the 1st/5th at Second Ypres and had previously fought in the Boer War; and William Davies, who lived at 6 Dickinsons Buildings, Parliament Street, and was killed at Gallipoli at the end of May 1915. As with the youngest, it is striking that the older men who died in action did so at the start of the war, mainly in 1915, again suggesting that the military became more careful about whom it put in the front line as the war progressed.

The geography of deaths: The streets and neighbourhoods

Reveille provides addresses for 80 per cent of the men listed. These are not always the addresses that the men lived in when they signed up: sometimes they are an address they had lived at before the war, sometimes they are their parents' address, and sometimes a widow's address after the war. In a few cases two or even three addresses are given. Nevertheless, these do provide an indication of the parts of the town that were most affected by deaths during the war. The image below (page 133) maps the numbers of deaths by street. It includes a 1919 map of Lancaster which shows that the street network in the centre of town has changed little over time except for the outward expansion of the town, and the demolition of houses and factories in a line from St. Leonard's Gate to Thurnham Street. The other thing to note is that this map both underestimates the extent of the losses experienced (we do not have addresses for 20 per cent of the men killed) and yet also overestimates it (we have more than one address for 13 per cent of the men listed). It may also be a little inconsistent in terms of which next of kin are listed with addresses and which are not.

Some clear patterns emerge from the map. Working from south to north, the worst affected areas were Primrose, to the east of the city centre, and close to the Barracks, which lost ninety-three men. Next, the area around St Leonard's Gate and Edward Street lost sixty-three. These two streets, where the housing has since been largely demolished and replaced with car parks, were the two worst affected streets in town with twenty-two and twenty losses respectively. North of here, the small area of terraced housing between Bulk Road and the canal around Green Street, lost fifty-four. Across the river, the southern part of Skerton around Lune Street lost forty-one; further north in Skerton, around Broadway and Main Street, seventy-five men were lost. Another area of note is the city centre: within what is now the one-way system where few people now live, eighty-seven men were lost.

One possible explanation for this pattern is that the war took a heavier toll on people in the poorer parts of town – many of these areas have terraced housing where the front doors open straight onto the street, or where housing has been demolished which may point to it being lower quality. While this theory is plausible, it needs to be treated with caution. Although we know how many

THE NATIONAL CONTEXT

The website The Long Long Trail (www.1914-1918.net/faq.htm) provides extensive data on the First World War, although any statistics, particularly on such a complex event, must be treated with caution. However, to put the local figures discussed here into a national perspective:

Britain entered the war with a much smaller standing army than those of France and Germany – in August 1914, it numbered just 733,514. In total, however, 8.7 million men served at some point of the war, just under 5 million drawn from the United Kingdom (the majority of whom from England) and the remainder from the Empire, including troops from India, Canada, Australia and Tasmania, New Zealand, South Africa, Newfoundland, West Indies and other Dominions. Around 62 per cent of these men served in France and Flanders on the Western Front. Other theatres of war included Mesopotamia, Egypt and Palestine, Salonika, Italy, and Gallipoli. The total of these men who died in action or of wounds, disease or injury, and including those missing presumed dead, number 956,703, of whom members of the Royal Navy and the Royal Flying Corps/Royal Air Force constitute 39,527. Around 27 per cent of the total casualties were from the Empire. About half of these men have named graves; the remainder are either buried but unidentifiable or lost (for example, at sea). The nature of warfare between 1914 and 1918 resulted in a high proportion of wounded men to men in action: the total number of British Army wounded in action was well over 2 million: these men could return to duty (62 per cent); return to limited roles (18 per cent); or be discharged (8 per cent). Around 7 per cent died of wounds received, but that figure does not include those who died of war-related injuries in the years following the war's immediate aftermath.

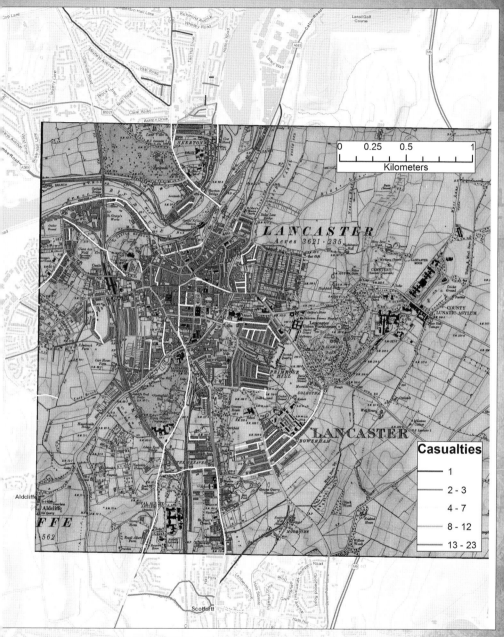

Casualties

—	1
—	2 - 3
—	4 - 7
—	8 - 12
—	13 - 23

Lancaster's losses by street. (Source: Casualty figures from Reveille. *The historic base map is a six inches to the mile map from 1919. For the modern base map, sources: Esri, HERE, DeLorme, Intermap, increment P Corp., GEBCO, USGS, FAO, NPS, NRCAN, GeoBase, IGN, Kadaster NL, Ordnance Survey, Esri Japan, METI, Esri China (Hong Kong), swisstopo, MapmyIndia, © OpenStreetMap contributors, and the GIS User Community.)*

people from a street were lost, we do not how many people lived on the street, so long streets of dense terraced housing with large numbers of people per house might have high numbers of losses simply because of the large number of people living on them.

One street of particular note is Green Street in Bulk. This had fifteen losses, the fifth highest, but, unlike other badly affected streets, is a short residential cul-de-sac. The odd-numbered side of this street, as it appears today, is shown in the following picture. The first door visible on the photograph is number 3, where Edward Clancy lived with his father. When he was killed on 26 April 1918 near Ypres, he became the last resident of the street to be killed. Staying on this side of the street, five doors further up, number 13 is listed as the address of both Hugh Rourke and James Muckalt. Hugh was killed on 13 March 1915, one of the first members of the 1st/5th Battalion to be killed in France. James was not killed until 12 April 1918 by which point he had served overseas for three-and-a-half years. A few doors further up, at number 21, Harold Dennison lived with his mother, a 'dependant widow,' until he was killed on 27 September 1917. Three doors further up, at number 27, William Butterworth was the first resident of the street killed on 18 October 1914. As previously described, the family lost three other brothers and their father during the war. Only three of the brothers are included in our figures, the other, Christopher, lived in Skerton. The houses at the end of the street have been demolished. The last one standing is number 33, however, on what is now a small patch of grass and a turning head, three neighbouring houses lost at least four people: Robert Cunliffe, from number 43, was

The *Lancaster Observer* reported on 7 May 1915 that twelve men from 6 Lucy Street had gone to war: 'two Bagots, five of Mrs Bettany's sons, two lads she had brought up, and three lodgers.' John Bagot was killed in June 1915, however, it appears that his brother and all of the Bettanys returned. Without their names, we cannot be sure of the fate of the 'two lads ... and three lodgers', however, a John Stevenson of 6 Lucy Street was killed on 7 January 1918.

killed with the 1st/5th at Frezenburg on 9 May 1915. Next door at number 45, Robert Shorrocks was killed when *HMS Cleopatra* hit a mine off of the Belgian coast on 4 August 1916. The ship was not badly damaged. His death came only six weeks after his brother Richard was killed fighting with Canadian forces. However, as he had emigrated to Canada before the war, he is not included as someone who lived on the street. Next door again, number 47, the last house on this side of the street, lost two men: Arthur Greenbank, killed on 6 November 1915, and George Yates, killed on 15 August 1916 with the 1st/5th on Lancaster's worst day of the Somme campaign. Turning round and coming back down the other side of the street, the highest house number was (and is) 32. John Condon lived here until he was killed at Loos on 26 September 1915 with the Seaforth Highlanders. Next door, the Young brothers, William and Robert, lived until they were killed on 27 November 1915 and 31 July 1917 respectively. Ten doors further down, at number 10, Peter Renshall seems to have gone to France with the 1st/5th in February 1915 and have survived both Second Ypres and the Somme before being killed near Ypres on 12 March 1917.

Thus a three-minute walk goes past thirty-nine houses from which fifteen men were recorded as lost, along with several

The odd-numbered side of Green Street today from numbers 3 to 33. The new houses at the end are on the far side of the canal. Photo taken from the junction with Bulk Road.

more that are slightly less directly connected with the properties. Although severe, the losses on this street are a microcosm of the way the war affected Lancaster. Some occurred in major events for the city such as Second Ypres, Loos and the Somme. Others are in lesser known events such as when HMS *Cleopatra* sustained minor damage hitting a mine, or dates like 6 November 1915 when, in the grand scheme of things, very little happened – unless you knew Arthur Greenbank.

As well as living in the town, the men who died also went to school and work. We have some information on this, although it is not as comprehensive as the data on addresses. We only know which school a casualty went to if it was named in his obituary. From this, we know the school that 442 casualties went to: 42 per cent of the total in the database. The casualties per school are shown in table 7.2. As these only refer to less than half of the casualties, school memorials or other records are likely to have more or different names and matching these names to the details on *Reveille* would be an interesting project that has yet to be done.

The first striking point about these statistics is the fact that schooling was spread around far more schools than today, many of which were small Anglican schools attached to churches. The worst affected school was the National School, or 'Nashy' which was at the east end of St Leonard's Gate where the retirement homes on St Leonard Court now stand. *Reveille* records eighty-one old boys who died. St Thomas', attached to St Thomas' Church on Marton Street in the city centre, lost fifty-five. Bowerham School, which remains on its wartime site, lost forty-nine.

We can also consider casualties in terms of their former places of work. The obituaries in *Reveille* provide employers for 456 men, a little under half of the total casualties. As with addresses, some give more than one employer, perhaps because they worked for more than one, or had worked for them at different times. These give a total of 492 employers. The largest losses were at the Lune Mills site, from where 137 men were killed. This site employed around 2,000 men and boys in the early 1900s suggesting that around 7 per cent of the workforce was killed. Given that we have occupations for less than half of the

Schools and Employers

School	Known deaths	% of known
National School	81	18.3
St. Thomas	55	12.4
Bowerham School	49	11.1
St. Peters	47	10.6
Christ Church	37	8.4
Skerton Council School	37	8.4
Lancaster Royal Grammar	32	7.2
Scotforth	16	3.6
Sulyard Street	14	3.2
St. Lukes	14	3.2
Friends School	12	2.7
St. Marys	10	2.3
Quay School	8	1.8
Greaves School	7	1.6
Ripley	6	1.4

Table 7.2 **Numbers of known casualties per school.**
The percentage column is the percentage of the 442 casualties for whom we have a known school. (Source: *Reveille*).

casualties, the real percentage could have been at least twice this. Storey's main site, White Cross Mills, which employed around 1,000 workers, lost forty-eight men. If we add casualties from the other sites owned by the two major employers, 180 casualties are known to have worked for Williamson's and sixty-seven for Storey's. In total, 54 per cent of the casualties with a known employer worked for one of these two companies.

The other major manufacturing employer was Waring and Gillow, whose major site still stands on St Leonard's Gate, which lost fourteen employees. The casualties reveal, however, that employment in Lancaster was about more than just manufacturing. As noted in Chapter 6, farmers were reluctant to let their sons go to war due to the labour shortages this would cause – despite this, twenty-one casualties are recorded as working in agriculture.

The Roll of Honour of the National School. (With thanks to Ripley St Thomas Church of England Academy)

Transport was another important employer: sixteen Lancastrian casualties worked for the London & North-Western Railway Company, which operated what is now the West Coast Mainline; a further five worked for Lancaster Castle station; another five worked for the Midland Railway which operated the line that ran from Morecambe, over what is now Greyhound Bridge to Lancaster Green Ayre station and then up what is now the Lune Valley cycle path, to eventually get to Leeds; and three more worked for the Lancaster and District Tramway Company which was based on Thurnham Street in the building which is now Kwik Fit. Many of the remaining casualties were divided among a wide variety of employers including Lancaster Corporation (seven deaths), the County Asylum (five), the Post Office (five), the police (four), Lancaster & District Cooperative Society (four), and the *Lancaster Guardian* (three). A lot also worked for small employers, perhaps most poignantly eleven men are recorded as working for 'his father'.

As with schools, these figures are underestimates based on obituaries. They could be enhanced by comparing these records with the many small memorials that still dot the town, for example, the memorial to Post Office workers records eight names rather than five, while the Cooperative Society's records five rather than four. Memorials to particular individuals still appear in places of employment around the town.

Conclusions

The statement that almost every family was affected by death in the war has become a cliché, albeit one that recent historians have attempted to challenge. What this chapter shows is that the impact of the war was undoubtedly devastating. The bald numbers, 1,055 men killed, 5.2 per cent of the male population, rising to 15 per cent in some age groups, do not do this justice. While we have some of the stories of the 134 brothers who were killed, we know little about the hundreds of parents who lost children, the wives left as widows, the children left without fathers, and all of the other family members who lost relatives. It does seem likely that anyone who was related to, lived near, worked, or had been to school with young(ish) men is likely to have known at least one, if not quite a number of people who were killed. If you walk down almost any street in town you will pass a house from which someone was lost.

Even this underestimates the impact. As previously stated, for every man killed, around three were wounded, often with devastating long-term consequences. Beyond this, the First World War foregrounded mental health issues associated with trauma. It is when shellshock, now termed post-traumatic stress disorder, began to be recognised as a medical condition. The impact of this, still poorly understood condition, on the men who came home and their families and friends can only be speculated on.

It is perhaps worth standing back from Lancaster briefly. J. Winter estimates that 1.6 per cent of the population of Britain and Ireland were killed. This makes Lancaster's experience of losing 2.6 per cent of its population significantly worse than average for Britain. In many countries – including Austria-Hungary, Bulgaria, France, Germany, Greece, Italy, the Ottoman Empire, Romania and Serbia – at least 3 per cent of the population, and in some cases many more, were killed. Lancaster's experience stands out in Great Britain, but was less severe than that of much of Europe.

8

THE END OF WAR AND REMEMBRANCE

The outbreak of peace was quietly anticipated in Lancaster by the start of November 1918. The press had reported on 2 November that 'The Hun Tide recedes' and on 9 November the chairman of the Lonsdale Appeal Tribunal looked forward to the diminution of work resulting from the request of several enemies for an armistice. The somewhat muted coverage of the press can perhaps be explained by the fact that the signing of the armistice was accompanied by an influenza epidemic. In October there had been fifty deaths attributed to influenza, with attempts made to maintain morale and avoid panic, for example, by closing schools and disinfecting public places of entertainment.

On 11 November, speaking at an impromptu meeting outside the Town Hall, Mayor Briggs spoke to the cheering crowds:

> I am delighted to announce that an armistice has been signed this morning at 5 o'clock, and that hostilities were to cease at 11 o'clock. (Cheers). Thus ends the greatest war of any age in a victory of Right over Might. (Renewed cheers.) Our hearts are overflowing with joy at the good news, and we have the

The influenza pandemic which broke out in 1918 affected *c.* 500 million people; 3 to 5 per cent of the world's population were killed. The *Lancaster Guardian* of 2 November reported the Mayor's expression of condolence at the losses to influenza: he mentioned specifically Mr Patterson, a Corporation official, who had lost his 11-year-old son and then 'within a day or two, also his Wife'.

right to rejoice, but let us not in the midst of our rejoicings forget those who have laid down their lives to help to win this war, and who have not laid them down in vain. (Cheers.)

The remainder of the day was observed as a general holiday. Services of thanksgiving followed. Local traders were quick to claim their place in the celebrations: the optician W.J. Hine (34 New Street) suggesting to the readers of the *Lancaster Guardian* that 'the only way to have peace in your sight, and comfort too, is to have properly made Spectacles or Eyeglasses.'

The press described how the 'thoroughfares were a blaze of colour with the hoisting of flags and banners, the Union Jack predominating. Sirens at the principal works were sounded,

Armistice Decoration on White Cross Mill Chimney, 1918. (LCM)

Float depicting 'Peace & Harmony'. (LCM)

141

Peace Day, Lancaster, 19 July 1919, showing uniformed men and women at the event. (KOM)

PEACE DAY K.O.R.L JULY 19.19.

The Presentation Tank standing outside of Lancaster Castle and the John O'Gaunt Gate. (LCM)

the church bells rang, and the streets were thronged by jubilant town people the majority of whom wore Union Jacks or brandished small flags.' The band of the 2nd Battalion, King's Own Royal Lancaster Regiment, with a detachment of troops, paraded the town, playing lively airs, and attracted several thousands of people to Dalton Square, the location of the Town Hall. At the same time, however, attention was turning to 'how we are to settle down comfortably and sensibly after the War' and rejoicing from the outset was combined with remembrance for the military war dead.

Although the armistice ended the fighting, the war was not brought to a formal conclusion until the signing of the peace treaties in 1919. In response, Lancaster held its Peace Celebrations complete with procession of floats representing all the major contributors to the war, a special medal presented to all school children and culminating in a rousing rendition of 'Rule Britannia' at the Giant Axe field.

A wide variety of local communities including church congregations, employers, schools and clubs displayed rolls of honour or plaques to their members. Most of these still remain. One exception is the presentation tank, Mark IV, which had stood on Castle Park from April 1920 in recognition of the contribution made by the town in War Bonds and Saving certificates: over £250,000.

Commemorating the dead

The greatest challenge was how to commemorate the men who would never return, given that their graves were dispersed across the globe. Some of Lancaster's war dead are commemorated multiple times at their places of work, worship and play. T. Bulmer & Co.'s *History, Topography and Directory of Lancaster and District*, published in 1912, lists twenty-seven churches, and nineteen academies and schools in Lancaster: these buildings came to house many of the local memorials. Other individuals may not be commemorated, notably men who died of war-related injuries after the unveiling of the war memorial and the men killed at the White Lund in October 1917, although Firth Dole, a works fireman killed in the fire, is listed in the Rolls of Honour in Nelson. Memorials to individuals had already been erected during the course of the war, although private shrines within houses have left little evidence outside such artefacts as crafted stands for the 'Dead Man's Penny', the memorial plaque issued to next-of-kin from 1919. For some, death could never be accepted. John Griffin was killed on 25 September 1915, one of Lancaster's worst days of the war. His great niece recalled how:

My nana's brother John Griffin (Charles St, Lancaster) was in the Seaforth Highlanders he was killed … at age 20 years. When his mum died, my great nana, it was discovered that she had kept all his clothes for years as she never gave up hope that he would one day return home. There was no closure because there was no body.

Even though the bodies of the fallen were not brought home, some were still included on the family grave stone. Private Joseph Thompson, 'Dear Joe', served with the Sherwood Foresters, and was killed in action on Monday, 4 November 1918, aged 22, after three years and eight months of service. Son of John and Dinah Thompson, of 35 Golgotha Road, Bowerham, he is commemorated with them in Scotforth Cemetery.

In other cases, memorials were raised to individuals who were killed. Perhaps the first of these in Lancaster was the plaque unveiled in Royal Lancaster Infirmary in December 1915 in memory of Captain Frank Miller Bingham. As well as being a doctor, Frank Bingham had played rugby and cricket, sang in Caton Church Choir and had been in the Territorials before the war in what became the 1st/5th Battalion, King's Own. He had survived the Second Battle of Ypres but was shot by a sniper on 22 May 1915 while reconnoitring the trenches that the battalion was to take over on its return to the front. He was 40 years old and left a wife and three children. Those entering the Infirmary's old building still walk past his memorial today.

Private Joseph Thompson's gravestone, Scotforth Cemetery. The inscription 'His precious life he gave' parallels the sacrifice of Jesus Christ with that of the soldier. (CPB)

Lancaster's First War Memorial? Frank Miller Bingham's plaque in the Royal Lancaster Infirmary. (KOM)

Lancaster already had one site established to commemorate the fallen of the King's Own: the Lancaster Priory which houses the Regimental Chapel. It was built in 1903–04 by moving part of the fifteenth century north wall twenty-one feet north and replacing it with four arches and an oak screen. The memorial was dedicated to the memory of the officers and men of all battalions who had died in the war in South Africa. After the First World War, a shrine containing a roll of honour to the fallen men of the regiment was unveiled by Field Marshal The Right Honourable Earl Haig on 27 November 1924.

> To provide the national context: Adrian Gregory points out that of the 5,930 memorials unveiled in Britain after the war, 5,151 had been erected by 1920. Only 2.2 per cent of British war memorials were sculptural. Over half – 57 per cent – were sited in places of worship.

On the north wall, just east of the Regimental Chapel, is a brass plaque to the members of the St John Ambulance Brigade who fell in the Great War. It includes five names, one of whom is the nurse Muriel Beatrice Ogilvy, who began her service aged 39 on 26 July 1915. She continued serving after the armistice, but died in November 1920. This is a rare inclusion of a woman on a war memorial in Lancaster, although the Bowerham Primary School Roll of Honour, unveiled by the

Field Marshal The Right Honourable Earl Haig on 27 November 1924. (KOM)

Lord Lieutenant of Lancashire, the Rightt Honourable Lord Shuttleworth on 8 July 1919, lists service as well as death, and includes six female names, distinguished by the inclusion of first names and by being colour coded.

Complementary war memorials

As in communities all across Britain, the armistice made topical discussions about appropriate physical memorialisation of the war for the community as a whole. Debates in Lancaster mirrored debates in the country as a whole in that there were two main competing visions as to what form that memorial should take: utilitarian or aesthetic. The utilitarian and less conventional possibility was the consequence of collaboration between local landscape architect Thomas Mawson and local industrialist Herbert Lushington Storey. Mawson's youngest son James Radcliffe had been killed in 1915. Shortly before his death, he had written to his father stating how moved he had been by the bravery of the injured men and asking his parents to do what they could to help the wounded. The idea for an industrial village to house disabled servicemen had appeared in Mawson's book *An Imperial Obligation,* first published in 1917 with a foreword by Field Marshal Sir Douglas Haig. Although the original idea was to create a chain of these across Britain, it was in Lancaster that Mawson's vision came to fruition.

Unlike Mawson, Herbert Storey's son came home safely; however the Storey family had a long history of philanthropic projects in Lancaster. Together, Storey and Mawson set up a committee to consider the erection of an industrial village to house disabled servicemen, which would act as a permanent memorial 'to the officers, non-commissioned officers and men of the King's Own Royal Lancaster Regiment and all those men and women of Lancaster and district who gave their lives in the service of their King and country during the Great War of 1914–1918.' The intention was to house and employ local men (with or without dependents) who had returned from the war with physical disabilities: the village itself would be part of their recovery, with its beautiful gardens, a bowling green and a club.

Meanwhile, the Town Council had set up a committee to discuss what form the local memorial should take, envisaging a more conventional monument. On 27 November 1918, the decision was taken at a public meeting held in the Town Hall to take both proposals forward. At the unveiling ceremony of the garden of remembrance, Alderman Nuttall was to comment on the two complementary war memorials: 'One had the noble ideal of helping the men who suffered and the other perpetuated the memory of the dead.'

There is photographic evidence that, in the interim, a temporary cenotaph reminiscent of that erected in Whitehall, London was erected in Dalton Square in the centre of the town opposite the Town Hall. On 3 December 1924, the Lancaster War Memorial was unveiled in the garden of remembrance attracting more wreaths, than *Lancaster Guardian* reported, then ever before. Designed by T.H. Mawson & Sons (which suggests the two memorial projects were not wholly antagonistic) it cost £1,900, and was paid for by public subscription from 'every class of the community … there being many small contributions from poor people'. Thirty-five feet in length, it consists of a stone background holding ten panels bearing the names of 1,010 men. In the centre is a bronze figure of Peace cast at the Bromsgrove School of Art. While the central figure was unveiled by the Mayor of Lancaster, four mothers who had lost twelve sons between them unveiled the panels: Mrs Butterworth, Mrs Gardner, Mrs Williams and Mrs Prickett. Every vantage point was taken by attendees, including 900 relatives and 300 subscribers. The *Lancaster Guardian* reported the address given by the Reverend J.W. Mountford which had reminded all who listened that the men listed on the memorial had:

'died to end war, and whether their dream was realised depended upon themselves. … They had done well to build the garden in the heart of the town. It would speak to their civic rulers, to their magistrates, and to all of

Although very poor quality, this is a rare piece of photographic evidence of Lancaster's temporary cenotaph: a young soldier or cadet stands on guard with arms reversed whilst dignitaries can be seen in the background on the steps of the Town Hall. (KOM)

ARMISTICE DAY DALTON SQUARE Nov 11 1924

unperishable things and would purify the soul of the town if was used properly and devoutly, and remembering why the names were on the panels.'

The number of dead was a matter of local pride, the press reporting: 'There were 1,010 names on the panels indicating that Lancaster men responded nobly and lost more heavily than many other towns by the war.' The validity of this claim has already been discussed in Chapter 7.

Meanwhile, on 5 November 1919, the foundation stone for the Westfield War Memorial Village was laid on the Westfield Estate donated by the Storey family. By the time the village was officially opened by Earl Haig in 1924, twenty-six cottages had been completed, housing seventy-two adults and fifty-one children in total. The rents were held artificially low. There had been multiple fundraising initiatives but, unlike the memorial in the garden of remembrance, the majority of the funding had come from leading local figures and businesses, as well as from the King's Own.

Westfield War Memorial Village may not have been a unique project for Industrial Settlements, but it is memorable for thriving to this very day. The village has been extended and modernised over time, and now has 113 properties (twenty-two of which are privately owned): priority is given to disabled ex-service personnel; regular and national service personnel; reservists; ex-merchant navy and support personnel; and their dependents. It still testifies to its memorial function in a number of ways: in its title; in the names given the houses; in the brass commemorative plaques inside the entrances to properties funded as a result of public donation (where these survive); and, more recently, in memorial gardens and a tree lit up with a light to represent each of the fallen. The first two cottages funded were named 'Leslie' and 'Morton' after the names of the two young men in whose

The Mayor of Lancaster, Councillor Briggs, Lord Derby and Earl Haig at the official village opening in 1924. (KOM)

Hilda Leyel
(1880-1957)

Hilda Leyel was an actress, political activist and renowned herbalist and author. She founded the *Society of Herbalists* (later the *Herb Society*) in England in 1927, and the Culpeper shops in London which sold herbal medicines, food and cosmetics. She was also a charity campaigner who permanently changed the face of charitable giving in Great Britain. Committed to helping disabled veterans and their families, Leyel devised a charity lottery, the winner of which would receive £25,000. Her first Golden Ballot had helped to fund one of Mawson's first industrial village projects at Preston Hall in Aylesford, Kent. The project permitted Preston Hall to continue as a centre for the treatment of tuberculosis and the establishment of a sanatorium, training colony and village settlement. The second Golden Ballot allowed Leyel to present the Westfield War Memorial Village in Lancaster with £20,000, which permitted twenty-one cottages to be erected, more than half of the original properties on Westfield. It also paid for the construction of roads, drainage and gates. The remaining £6,000 of her donation was invested in War Stock, with continued development in the village funded from the interest. Leyel's fundraising activities had attracted the attention of the state, however, and Leyel was prosecuted for the running of an illegal lottery. Luckily, as a young Society hostess in Lincoln's Inn she had made some influential friends, aided no doubt by her refined tastes in food and wine. She opted for trial by jury in 1922, arguing that the ballot had been run purely for charitable purposes, and had transformed the lives of many veterans. The case against her was overturned, and such fundraising initiatives for charitable causes have been deemed legal in the United Kingdom ever since. In the Westfield War Memorial Village, four conjoined houses still bear the name Leyel Terrace.

Hilda Leyel (1880–1957). (Reproduced with kind permission from the Herb Society Archive)

Jennie Delahunt's monument in her studio. (KOM)

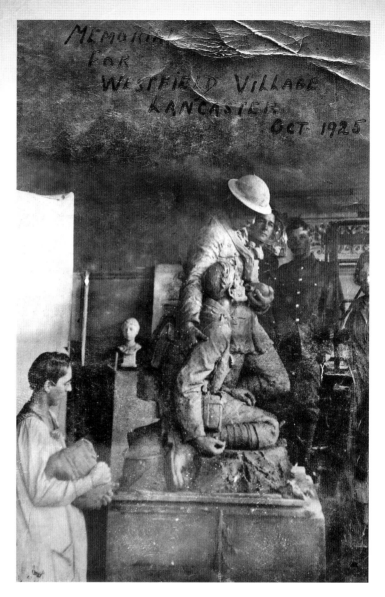

memory they had been built. Subsequent dwellings were more likely to be named after specific battles, such as Ypres and Le Cateau, Gallipoli and Somme – regimental battle honours in which the King's Own had suffered large numbers of casualties.

The official war memorial in Westfield Village is held in the communal room, however there is a striking monument at the heart of the village, thanks to Herbert Storey's intervention. Initially the plot in the village centre was reserved for a sundial, as befitted the feel of an English village, but in May 1924, Herbert Storey proposed a figurative monument representing a soldier giving a wounded comrade a drink. He was to get his way. The sculptress was Jennifer (Jennie) Delahunt, a Lancaster artist, about whom little is known, except that she was born on 16 April 1876, trained at the Manchester School of Art, and worked 'in joint services' at the School of Art at the Storey Institute and the Girls' Grammar School, where she taught from its foundation in August 1907 to July 1934. She may be seen on the right a rare photograph of her studio (opposite): the sitters for the monument posing behind the statue. The memorial was unveiled in 1926 and is still the focal point of the village today.

The monument at the heart of Westfield War Memorial Village today. (CPB)

Memorialising the fallen today

The memorialisation of the First World War in Lancaster continued into the next century. In 2002 the Lancaster Military Heritage Group began a War Memorial Project, the intention of which was to research the lives of the men and women listed on the local war memorials of Lancaster and Morecambe. That research was presented in *The Last Post: The War Memorials of Lancaster and Morecambe* and the *Reveille* website which was recently revised in a project with the Department of History and the School of Computing and Communications at Lancaster University supported by the Heritage Lottery Fund. 'Streets of Mourning' maps Lancaster's war dead on to the addresses listed in the obituaries of the fallen – where the men or their loved ones lived. Members of the local community shared stories of their ancestors and showed how the impact of the First World War has

Shrigley and Hunt are nearly forgotten today, but were one of the leading stained glass manufacturers of the late nineteenth century. The business began in the 1750s, but became known as Shrigley and Hunt in 1878, with premises still discernible as such on Castle Hill, Lancaster, opposite the John O'Gaunt gate. The online database of war memorials lists twenty memorial windows accredited to this local firm after the First World War. These are mainly located in the North West.

ricocheted down the generations. One moving contributor was Ian Birnie, the great-grandson of William Butterworth, the oldest of the four Butterworth brothers listed on Lancaster's war memorial. In October 2014, Ian attended the funeral of his great-grandfather, whose remains had been found alongside those of fourteen other British soldiers, close to the village of Beaucamps-Ligny, near Lille. The soldiers were reburied with full military honours at a Commonwealth War Graves Commission cemetery in Bois-Grenier. As Ian noted, 'When we were told that it was William, it was almost as if we'd lost someone only yesterday. It seems ridiculous as this happened 100 years ago, but to me, and to our family, this is a loss.'

Commemoration of the First World War has not ended in the City. Global Link's 'Documenting Dissent' project has used the skills of local volunteers to recover various underre-searched aspects of Lancaster's experience of the First World War, from conscientious objection to the munition workers and more. More conventional memorialisation also continues with Lancaster's first Victoria Cross (VC) won by Second Lieutenant James Leach, who was serving with the 2nd Manchester Regiment (see Chapter 2). He was awarded the VC for his 'conspicuous bravery' for recapturing a trench from the Germans at Festubert. James Leach was born at Bowerham Barracks, and attended Bowerham School from July 1897 to July 1901. The school grounds were chosen to house the commemo-rative paving stone: unveiled in 2016. In the same year, three new roads were named after distinguished service men of the King's Own: 2nd Lieutenant Ronald Macdonald MC, Private Reginald Sydney Dennison MM and Captain Albert Ellwood MC. Thus, 100 years later it continues to be true: the end of the war was only the beginning of its commemoration.

SECOND LIEUTENANT
JAMES LEACH
THE MANCHESTER REGIMENT
29TH OCTOBER 1914

*Memorial stone to
Second Lieutenant
James Edgar Leach,
VC, and in the
Remembrance Garden
at Bowerham Primary
and Nursery School.
(CPB)*

FURTHER READING

Britain and the First World War:

Braybon, G., *Women workers in the First World War: The British Experience* (London: Croom Helm, 1981)

DeGroot, G.J., *Back in Blighty: The British at Home in World War One* (London: Vintage, Rev Upd edition 2014)

Gregory, A., *The Last Great War: British Society and the First World War* (Cambridge University Press, 2008)

Hayes, J., *The Enemy Within: Picturing, Confronting and Confining the 'Alien' in Lancaster and Morecambe during the First World War* (Lancaster University, 2016)

Panayi, P., *The Enemy in Our Midst : Germans in Britain during the First World War*. (New York: Berg, 1991)

Winter, J., *The Great War and the British People. 2nd edition.* (London: Palgrave, 2003)

Lancaster during the War:

Fidler, J., *Lancaster in the Great War* (Barnsley: Pen & Sword, 2016)

Gooderson, P.J., *Lord Linoleum: Lord Ashton, Lancaster and the Rise of the British Oilcloth and Linoleum Industry* (Keele: Keele UP, 1996).

Graves, R., *Goodbye to All That* (London: Penguin, 2000) (Robert Graves' 1929 autobiography, which includes an account of his time as a guard at the Lancaster Carriage and Wagon Works on Caton Road)

Harrison, P., *Lancaster Girls' Grammar School. The First Century ... Continuity and Change* (Martin Print & Design, 2006)

Shevin-Coetzee, M., and Coetzee. F., *Commitment and Sacrifice: Personal Diaries from the Great War* (Oxford University Press, 2015) (includes a reprint of the diary of Willy Wolff who was interned at the Caton Road Wagon Works and Knockaloe)

www.britainfromabove.org.uk/sites/default/files/06%20The%20

National%20Factory%20Scheme%20List.pdf (describes National Factory Scheme)

www.documentingdissent.org.uk (for fascinating coverage of various dimensions of Lancaster's experience at war)

Lancaster on the eve of the War:

lancastercivicsociety.files.wordpress.com/2014/06/canalside-mills-c. docx ('Lancaster's Canalside Mills' [Lancaster Civic Society Leaflet 21])

Winstanley, M., *A History of Lancaster, 1193–1993* (Keele: Ryburn/ Keele University Press, 1993) (see pp145–198, Chapter: 'The town transformed, 1815–1914')

www.archaeologyuk.org/lahs/Contrebis/20_39_Price.pdf (Lancaster Archaeological and Historical Society's 'Contrebis' journal, Volume 20, 1995, 'Industry And Changes In Its Location In Nineteenth Century Lancaster')

Military history and casualties:

Cowper, J.M., *The King's Own: The story of a royal regiment. Volume III. 1914-1950*. (Aldershot: Gale & Polden, 1957)

Gregory, I.N., & Peniston-Bird, C.M., *The First World War: Commemoration and Memory*. (London: Routledge, 2017)

Hodgkinson, A., *The King's Own, 1/5th Battalion, TF in the European War, 1914–1918*. (Lancaster: King's Own Royal Regiment Museum, 2005)

MacDonald, L., *1915: The death of innocence* (London: Penguin, 1997), (contains vivid accounts of what both Second Ypres and Loos would have been like for ordinary soldiers)

wp.lancs.ac.uk/greatwar (provides online access to *Reveille, Streets of Mourning, Lancaster in the Great War: Community Memories* and the *Great War Trail App*)

www.kingsownmuseum.com/ww1.htm *(King's Own Royal Regiment Museum website)*

www.lancasterwarmemorials.org.uk (provides online access to *Reveille*)

www.longlongtrail.co.uk/battles/battles-of-the-western-front-in-france-and-flanders/the-battle-of-loos (provides statistics from the war and a more factual description of the Battle of Loos)

About the Authors

IAN GREGORY is Professor of Digital Humanities in the Department of History at Lancaster University. He mainly works on how computer technology, especially mapping technologies, can be used to better understand the past. As well as work on the First World War he works on projects involving a wide range of digitised historical sources including historical newspapers, public health reports, census data and Lake District literature. He has published four other books: *Troubled Geographies: A spatial history of religion and society in Ireland*; *Toward Spatial Humanities: Historical GIS and Spatial History*; *Historical GIS: Technologies, methodologies, scholarship*; and *A Place in History: A Guide to Using GIS in Historical Research*. He has also published numerous journal articles and book chapters.

CORINNA PENISTON-BIRD is a senior lecturer in cultural and gender history in the Department of History at Lancaster University. Since 1998, her research and teaching has centred on gender dynamics in Britain in the world wars, with a particular interest in the relationship between memories and cultural representations, and on the emphases and omissions of war memorials. She is currently working on gendered commemoration, with a particular focus on British war memorials. Previous publications include, with Penny Summerfield, *Contesting Home Defence: Men, Women and the Home Guard in the Second World War* (Manchester: Manchester University Press, 2007) as well as three edited collections and numerous articles.